Empower Your Life

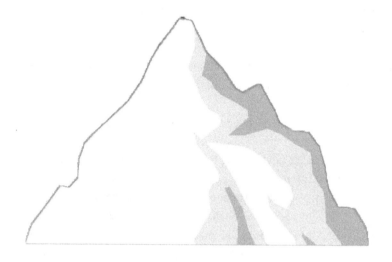

Discover Your Strengths,
Release Your Fears,
Follow Your Heart

Powerful You!
PUBLISHING
Sharing Wisdom ~ Shining Light

EMPOWER YOUR LIFE
Discover Your Strengths, Release Your Fears, Follow Your Heart

Copyright © 2018

Published by: Powerful You! Inc. USA
powerfulyoupublishing.com

Library of Congress Control Number: 2018932141

Sue Urda and Kathy Fyler – First Edition

ISBN: 978-0-9970661-7-3

First Edition March 2018

Self Help / Women's Studies

Printed in the United States of America

Dedication

*This book is dedicated to those
who seek, discover, and share
their personal power for the highest good
of themselves and others.*

Table of Contents

Foreword

How empowered are you really? The path to our personal power rises up from a series of life events and actions, or a life altering situation that plunges us into a new self-awareness, possibly a transformation. We may find ourselves led in a new direction or enterprise. Once you experience being empowered, you feel good, calm, purposeful, and with a knowing that you're on the right path and in alignment with you. To live an empowered life is to invest in you and in the paths of your destiny with conviction and control.

Life frequently asks or demands us to step up and push beyond our limits and beyond what we consider even possible. In "Empower Your Life" you'll meet authors whose enduring strength and power grew from stumbling blocks and hurdles they had to overcome. Like us, they often didn't know or recognize their capabilities or inner strength until it was tested. And each author's remarkable and moving pathway to embrace and live their personal power is distinctive and noteworthy.

In these candid and soul-searching stories, healers, coaches, instructors, consultants, speakers, spiritual channels, and entrepreneurs share their transformations and how they unearthed their unique empowerment. They light a path for us to claim our own personal power and often give us tools and techniques to guide us.

Each author discovered her power in a different, yet affirmative way. You'll find out what happens when we acknowledge and release core wounds and beliefs that diminish our self-worth. Trusting and listening to the quiet prodding of your heart, as one healer discovered, created reality on her own terms. One author's suicidal thoughts awakened her desire to live and reclaim her family, and open to more self-loving. Once they heroically ventured into seeing themselves differently and acted on that new awareness, their lives were more fulfilling, joyful and on track. And yours can be too.

As we share their journey, their stories also empower us. Sometimes painful, always awakening, and often transformative, they emerge into a new way of being in the world and with themselves. And we do too. They offer us hope and an understanding that we too can gather our courage and forthrightness to live more fully and contentedly. Whether it's responding with authority and confidence to events, circumstances and people, healing a deep emotional or core wound that's festered for years, regaining health and acceptance from an illness or injury that refused to abate, or following your dreams and taking risks based on your inner guidance, YOU can live more powerfully.

In these compelling revelations we also discover what can lead us to a more fulfilling life. We can breathe easier knowing that the way to empowerment, as these authors confess, isn't by perfection or overnight. It often takes bumping into mountainous circumstances and up against people with destructive intent, and even derailing, to come to a place of self-acceptance and self-understanding.

Empowerment is feeling strong and in charge of our lives, and more often than not, with confidence and courage. It's having control over our feelings, thoughts and actions. Empowerment isn't accomplished in a moment. Being empowered beckons us to make conscious choices that support us, without detracting from or unfavorably impacting another's life. What is so wonderful is that these authors expanded their understanding of self-empowerment. They chose to give back in some way to teach and help other people like us claim or reclaim ourselves and live in the recognition of our vastness. One author's journey led to creating outdoor retreats for youth to experience the limitless teachings of empowerment through nature. While another's nonprofit organization brings deeper meaning and comfort to dying people and to their loved ones.

The ultimate Feel Good Guidess is of course Sue Urda, an Award-Winning and #1 Bestselling Author, and Co-Founder of Powerful You! Publishing and Powerful You! Women's Network.

She's helped more than 300 women achieve their dreams of being published authors. Sue is an authentic mentor, speaker, inspirer and leader whose passion is helping and connecting women for business, personal and spiritual growth. She assists women "to *find the feel good* and live in that space every day."

I've had the infinite pleasure of working with Sue. As a co-author in another one of her inspiring books, on podcasts and radio shows, and growing together in friendship and mutual respect. Sue's loving, generous and caring nature is infused in everything she does. One of her impressive features is her ability to live and practice what she teaches: A life built by conscious design and in dedicated service to the empowerment of others. Sue's a cheerleader and entrepreneur who along with her partner, Kathy Fyler, connects and empowers people and helps raise the vibration of people and the planet.

Kathy Fyler is an Amazon #1 bestselling author and teacher, and the other half of Powerful You! Network and Publishing, whom I've also worked with throughout the publishing and podcast process. She makes it all run smoothly with her experience and passion for technology and people. Kathy expertly assists women to create sustainable connections via the internet, in-person meetings and in publishing. Sue and Kathy beautifully complement one another and every book, meeting, retreat, and encounter they've created is built on respect, love, and understanding.

This book is no exception. You have a premier seat and are invited to witness the awakening and transformation process of other women like yourself and gain wisdom and courage from the messages they genuinely impart. Their stories will shift you, encourage and arouse your desire to live your truth and consciously assert your infinite power. Why not now?

Dr. Jo Anne White
Amazon #1 International Bestselling, Award Winning Author & Speaker, Certified Coach & Consultant, & Energy Master Teacher
Read more about Jo Anne on page 133.

Introduction

What is the dominating thought you have as you turn the pages and begin to read the words in this book? Most people have questions. Will I enjoy these stories? Will I learn anything? How will I feel after reading these personal accounts? What's here for me? These may be the first thoughts that cross your mind when something new is in front of you—so you might be wondering what is between the covers of this book that you are now holding.

Or you might be wondering how a book like this comes together. More accurately, you may wish to know how a group of women from the United States, Canada, and Nigeria—many who don't even know each other and may never even meet in person—have conspired to bring forth such a book.

You might wonder why they would bare their souls, expose their secrets, and show you their flaws.

You might ask who would share such deeply personal and sometimes unflattering truths about themselves. Who would air their 'dirty laundry' or put themselves up for possible ridicule, judgment, and scrutiny? Why go there if you don't have to? Why not keep it tucked away in a closet somewhere and go on living your life?

The answer is simple…

These women have stepped into their power; and they now feel a great need and desire to help others do the same.

As you read the stories you will see the raw emotion and unbridled heart of each author. You will share in her joys and pain; you will laugh, cry, and celebrate with her. Her story may reflect your own, and through her transformation, you will gain insights and strength, courage, inspiration, and perhaps even freedom.

Mostly, you may see yourself in some of these stories. These are ordinary women who have transformed their circumstances into something personally extraordinary. The evidence is in the lives they live today.

It takes a village, not only to raise a child, but to raise ourselves into the women we would have ourselves become.

It is the wish and intent of these authors to be truthful with themselves and others so that they may move forward powerfully in life, having learned and grown from their mistakes, triumphs, and experiences—and if *they* can do it, *you* can too! Many of these authors have careers and businesses that focus on assisting other women to empower themselves, and all of them have chosen to share their story in the hopes of helping someone like you along the way.

It is said that you must first release the past before you can fully live the potential for your life. We believe this to be true.

Allow yourself to become immersed in these heartfelt and raw stories and learn the lessons that are shared through these words of truth—they may help you to move forward from the beliefs that hold you back. In these stories you will find comfort, guidance, and joy—and surely, you will find hope. May the stories of these authors serve as a beacon of strength for your journey.

It is our intention and purpose to be a source for good and to do our part in raising consciousness, compassion, and the "feel good factor" of people and the planet. This book contributes to this purpose.

Know above all that you can be, do, and have anything you desire. These women are living proof. And if you ever need encouragement or inspiration, flip through this book, open to any page, and read. Your heart will open and expand.

With much love and gratitude,
Sue Urda & Kathy Fyler
Co-Founders of Powerful You! Inc.

Go Deep...

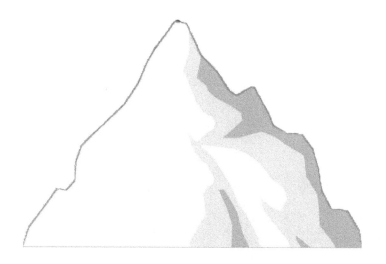

That's Where the
Treasure Lies

Navigating Your River of Life
Susie Kincade

Schloop... schloop...schloop. The sound of the oar blades pushing through emerald water sets a steady rhythm that I match with my own body. Leaning right, then left on the oars, I use my weight to add force to each confident stroke as my fourteen-foot rubber boat, Mni Wiconi, glides across the glassy surface of the Colorado River. The name means Water is Life in Lakotah, and indeed I never feel more alive than when I am on the river.

Nearby, my fifteen companions in seven other rafts move to their own tempo. I hear snippets of conversations and laughter skipping across the river's smooth surface like flat stones. A canyon wren serenades us, its trill of tweeeeeet, tweeet, tweet cascading down the vertical red walls. Five hundred feet above us an eagle soars on air currents formed where red rock meets pale blue sky.

I scan Mni, checking the load with satisfaction. She's snugly fitted with everything I need for an eighteen-day, 225-mile trip: a giant cooler; dry bags with camping gear, food, maps, guidebooks, and my wooden flute; twelve gallons of water; a table, rescue gear, first aid, and two spare oars. I'm ready for anything, because anything can happen on the river.

Rounding a bend, my heart beats faster as I hear the rushing roar of white water. It is House Rock Rapid, the first major cataract of the trip. The boatmen signal each other, pull into a quiet eddy on the left side of the river, then tie up and climb to a high vantage point where we can look down on the rapid and scout our course. A shiver of excitement races through me.

The Grand Canyon rates its rapids on a difficulty scale of 1 to 10. House Rock is a 7. The water pounds down the upper part then drives into a deep "hole," a depression in the surface caused by a rock deep below. Then it explodes into a huge boat-eating lateral wave coming off the left side canyon wall. With the force of the mighty Colorado River driving toward that hole, I must be precise in how I enter the rapid and row with intensity and power, or I'll be drawn into a boat-flipping disaster.

Together we review the run, giving ourselves a series of instructions and reminders. Enter on the glassy tongue just right of the middle. Keep a forty-five-degree angle facing the left wall, pulling away from it. Pull, pull, pull!! If I accidentally hit that lateral wave, make sure to hit it straight on, at ninety degrees; otherwise it will turn the boat sideways, I'll slide into the hole and the wave will crash over me, likely flipping the boat. I know the lesson well. I learned it the hard way.

Twenty years and four Grand Canyon trips before, I was on this stretch of river with my former husband and many of these same friends. It wasn't just any vacation: our marriage was in trouble and I looked forward to long days on the river, talking through our issues, finding our way back to each other.

I was experienced on the river but not behind the oars. The flat sections didn't scare me, but I was petrified of the rapids. Neither I nor my husband had been down the Grand, but I knew its rapids were some of the biggest, most powerful in the world. Before the trip I'd read "Death on the Grand Canyon," a morbid if cautionary anthology of horrific accidents, deaths, and disappearances that have occurred. I had also rewritten my will and wrote sealed letters to my daughters, ages six and eight, just in case.

Our trip began as planned. Everything was exciting and new, and though the conversations I'd longed for hadn't happened yet, I remained hopeful. I was rowing, following the other boats through the flatwater, when we came around the bend above House Rock Rapid. We were heading straight for it!

"Here, take the oars!" I shouted to my husband over the roar of the whitewater.

"No, you row it," he replied.

"But I can't. I'm not ready. I don't know how. PLEASE, take the oars!"

"It's too late to switch now. Just keep it straight. You'll be fine."

I had no choice. "Keep it straight, keep it straight," I chanted to myself as we rushed down the tongue. I looked left and right. The boat was in perfect parallel alignment with the canyon walls.

Okay, this must be okay, I thought.

It wasn't.

The massive, curling wave careened off the wall and slammed into the left side of the boat, hijacking it and plunging us into the hole backwards. I flew off the back and down into the icy water. Fierce whirlpools grabbed at my legs, pulling me deeper.

I saw my air bubbles going up and thought, *This is it! This is the part where I die!*

My next thought was, *Or I could save myself and swim to the surface.*

I erupted into frothy whitecaps and grabbed the safety line on the boat, which miraculously hadn't flipped and was bobbing beside me. My husband rowed us to shore and I dragged myself onto the sand, still coughing up river water. A heated exchange followed. You didn't keep it straight! Yes, I did! Not to the wave! Huh? You didn't tell me that part! You should have known. But I told you I wasn't ready; that I didn't want to do it!

He reached into the bow of the boat and pulled out the inflatable kayak we'd planned to use in the calmer sections of the river. He grabbed the pump and began inflating it.

"What are you doing?" I asked, the panic turning my words shrill.

"I'm having my own river trip."

"What am I supposed to do?"

Without answering, he took his paddle and pushed off in the kayak, paddling toward the group that had assembled on the bank below us.

That moment, as I climbed, shaking, into the rower's seat and began a new journey as captain of my own boat, I knew three things: 1) Our relationship was permanently damaged, 2) I had faced my fear of dying and realized I had some say in the matter, and 3) I was still going to need some help getting down the river.

That night at camp, my husband remained adamant about paddling the river in the kayak. Jerry, a river guide and geologist from our group, offered to help me. He had a broken thumb and couldn't row but he would ride along and coach me down the river.

In the days that followed, Jerry taught me how to read the water, to feel and use the nuances of currents, to dance with the river, rather than force my way through.

I learned to scout rapids, discern obstacles, find my "line" and envision my run. When the fickle river or a blast of wind took me off my course, I learned to adjust, be flexible. I began to listen…to the river, to the rocks, the wind, to my own instincts, and trust what I heard.

By embracing the river and her mysteries, I traded fear for respect and excitement. Each day, my courage and confidence grew. I was alert, ready for the unexpected, eagerly anticipating what was around the next bend.

In the quiet times, as we floated through the stone cathedral of Time, Jerry told me the geologic story of the Grand Canyon. I began to see the massive layered walls of the gorge through new eyes. Four billion-year-old granite rose up in mesmerizing patterns of pink, black, gray, and white; the fiery earth's core captured in stone. I recognized the infinitesimal role that my life and its dramas play in the great layers of time. I felt my spirit move into a quiet place of surrender and awe.

Paradoxically, I realized that no matter how small and inconsequential I may feel in the grand scheme of Time, I am here, and a vital part of the vast web of life. As that, I am significant and what I bring to that web matters, whether it's on a river adventure or in my family, community, or work.

At the end of our eighteen-day trip, I emerged from the canyon inspired, empowered, and standing firmly in my confidence, self-trust, resilience, and self-worth.

Six years later, when my husband finally abandoned our family, I was put to the test again.

Falling into the abyss of my divorce was like a slow-motion repeat of the moment I fell out of my boat at House Rock Rapid. As I plunged into dark, tumultuous rapids of my husband's betrayal, the mighty whirlpools of victimhood and self-pity sucked me under and threatened to suffocate me.

Where was the strong woman and fierce competitor who had rowed the Grand Canyon, climbed mountains, tried out for the Olympics, and raised two children, at one point while living in a tipi? Was this going to be the end for her?

Once again, I decided to swim to the surface.

Like on that first Grand Canyon trip, I needed guidance to navigate these uncharted, stormy waters. And I found many wonderful guides who helped me build upon the lessons I'd learned on the river. My trip down the Canyon had taught me that everything I need is already within me, and my guides helped me learn to listen, trust, and transform my life.

I began this part of my journey by undertaking a three-year study to re-discover and embody the Divine Feminine and balance the masculine/feminine energy within. My vows upon graduation: to serve the Earth, Women, and Girls.

Next, I earned my International Certification as a Nature-connected Coach. Now I lead exciting nature-adventure retreats for empowering girls and women. As we paddle the river, rock-climb, and hike in Colorado's Rocky Mountains, I guide clients to their courage, resilience, inner wisdom, and self-trust. I teach them empowering skills and practices to build their inner strength, and have helped hundreds of women and girls discover, as I did, that they could navigate their own river of life.

One day, Susan, a repeat client, called to tell me of a breakthrough. "You know, I've been eddied out for months since my mom died," she confided. "I just wasn't ready to get back into the current. Then my first grandchild was born, and I picked up my paddle and roared back into my river of life!"

Another client, a devoted, loving, wonderful mom, struggled with letting go of her children as they entered high school. She was working so hard to help them be successful, setting up study programs, managing their activities, and preparing healthy meals. Yet, the more she offered the more demanding they got, calling her to bring their forgotten homework or permission slips to school, demanding that she wash their sportswear for the next day's practice, and generally running roughshod over her.

I asked her to close her eyes and remember the times we were on the river together, specifically what it felt like when she turned her boat upstream and paddled like mad against the current.

"That was impossible," she recalled. "I think that's what I'm doing now and it's just not sustainable."

I agreed. "Are you alone in your boat?"

She paused for a beat, then exclaimed, "Oh my gosh! I see it. I need to put these kids in their own boat! They're ready to paddle their own river!"

Coaching moments like these remind me that I am doing my small part in the web of life to make it stronger and empowering others to make it stronger too.

Now, standing above House Rock Rapid, listening to it roar below me, I smile, remembering the transformation that began for me at this spot, and all I've learned from it. Then, my heart thumping with respect, gratitude, and just the right amount of adrenaline, I scout my line.

I see it. I feel it. It's time to run it.

ABOUT THE AUTHOR: Susie founded Women's Empowerment Workshop in 2009 to empower girls and women of all ages and ability with courage, confidence, and self-awareness. In her unique, nature-connected coaching programs, nature is both the metaphor and the medium to help clients discover their personal power. An aspiring Olympic athlete, Susie was the first woman to compete on a men's varsity collegiate athletic team, diving for UCLA in 1972-74. An avid outdoor adventurer who innately understands the power of our connection to the natural world, Susie is a personal coach in Vail, Colorado, a trained ceremonialist, Awakening the Dreamer facilitator with the Pachamama Alliance, and TEDxVailWomen speaker.

Susie Kincade
Women's Empowerment Workshop
womenempower.us
susie@womenempower.us
970-328-5472

Empowering to the End
Death Through the Eyes of a Doula
Janie Rakow

Death. It's a natural part of life, yet we still feel uncomfortable using the word, instead favoring euphemisms like "crossed over", "departed", "expired" and "entered eternal peace." It wasn't always this way. A hundred years ago, we didn't run from death. People died in their homes. People were waked in their homes. Relatives, friends, and villages came together, celebrating the person who died. As we became more medically and technologically advanced, we lost our relationship with death; we became a death-phobic society. It was this disconnect that would lead me to find my calling as an end of life doula.

I'm not a doctor. I'm not a nurse. In fact, I have no medical background at all. I'm not even a social worker or a chaplain, though I utilize some of the same skills. I'm an end of life doula, a person that provides emotional, spiritual, and physical support to dying people and their families. We also help lift the veil so we can speak openly and honestly about death.

One of my roles is helping our patients create legacy and meaning during those final months of life. When a terminal illness strikes, we get so caught up in the physical and emotional pain that the human aspect often gets lost. Each one of us has walked on this earth for years, living full lives surrounded by loved ones. What has your life meant? Who have you touched? How can your memories live on after you die?

End of life doulas have those difficult talks with people about their death. Where do they want to die? In the bedroom surrounded by loved ones? One of my patients was from the United Kingdom and loved soccer; he wanted soccer matches playing on the TV while he was dying. Another patient loved to cook. Her hospice bed was set up near the kitchen of her home so she could smell her favorite foods cooked by her loving daughters as she was dying. What kind of music do they want to hear? My mom loved Broadway tunes, so that's what I played for her when she took her last breath.

Given my career choice, one might think I grew up around death, but this wasn't the case. Other than my grandparents, all of whom died at ripe old ages, I didn't encounter much death while growing up. To me, it was a natural event that occurred after a long, well-lived life. At least that is what I thought until I was twenty-five.

Back then I was a young CPA, just three years out of college. I was on a business trip in Atlantic City when I got the news. My childhood best friend, who was also leaving on a business trip, was hailing a cab in NYC when a garbage truck snagged her overnight bag and pulled her under the truck. She was instantly killed. I remember sitting in my hotel room, in shock, unable to believe someone so young and so close to me had died.

Grieving not only turns your world upside down, it can make you question everything. Why did she die so young? Is she somewhere in an afterlife? Where is God in all this? In search of these answers, I began reading every book I could find on death and dying. Elizabeth Kubler-Ross, Shirley MacLaine, Victor Frankl. I didn't know it then, but my friend's death would lead me to my calling.

Several years into this quest, I began reading a book about hospice. I was deeply moved by the stories of hospice volunteers who visited terminally ill patients and provided them with companionship and support. That book would become the catalyst for change in my own life. Burnt out and tired from the rat race, I was looking for something purposeful. I quit my job and signed up to volunteer at my local hospice.

For several years, I was a friendly volunteer, meaning I worked with patients who were sick but I didn't necessarily see them die. Then, in 2008, I heard about a small niche program at my hospice, and though I had never heard the phrase "end of life doula" before,

I was intrigued. The training, conducted by end-of-life pioneer Henry Fersko-Weiss, would teach me how to help people facing death. It would also lead to the life transformation I had been seeking.

Shortly after becoming a doula, I began to notice a funny thing: my patients and their families were touching my heart as much as I was touching theirs. Friends said, "This must be so depressing for you, dealing with death all the time," but it was actually quite the opposite. Being able to help people at such an intimate time, and witnessing the love, heartache, and compassion, was both humbling and awe-inspiring.

These families would inevitably ask why they had never heard of an end of life doula. Why wasn't this work done all over the country? Their aunt in Florida needed a doula, their cousin in California needed help with a dying brother. Could we assist? Did we know a doula or a hospice that had a doula in another state? Unfortunately, the answer was usually no.

To fill this overwhelming need, in 2015 Henry Fersko-Weiss and I formed The International End of Life Doula Association (INELDA), a non-profit dedicated to training people to be end of life doulas and enabling hospitals, hospices, and organizations to have an end of life doula program. Doulas can be people in the medical profession, social workers, or anyone who has an open heart, good listening ear, and a desire to be of service.

There are dozens of incredible stories I could tell, but the one that sticks out most in my mind is that of Sam, a forty-year-old man, and his wife Lucy. Four years earlier, Sam had been eating Chinese food when he noticed his hands couldn't grasp the chopsticks. The symptoms progressed and a few months later he was diagnosed with amyotrophic lateral sclerosis (ALS), the progressive neurodegenerative disease that afflicted baseball great Lou Gehrig and physicist and author Stephen Hawking. ALS is a nasty disease. It often starts in the hands, feet, or limbs, and eventually spreads throughout the entire body, affecting all voluntary muscles, so you can no longer move or speak. The cruelest part of this disease is that your mind is fully intact and you can still feel pain. By the time I met Sam, he was in the hospital, hooked up to a BiPAP machine and unable to breathe on his own.

INELDA had recently trained a group of doulas at the hospital where Sam was a patient. When his palliative care team told Lucy about us, she welcomed the help. Nurses, social workers, and chaplains are wonderful, but their plates are full with patients and paperwork. This means a lot of the minute-to-minute care falls to the family. The doulas are there to fill these gaps.

Our doula team was told that Sam communicated using Morse code, blinking the dots and dashes with his eyes. Knowing that at some point he would no longer be able to speak, he'd memorized the entire Morse code alphabet! That way, he'd still be able to "talk" when he lost the physical ability. Since our team didn't know it, we taped the Morse code chart to the wall behind Sam's bed. A quick blink was a dot, and a slow blink was a dash. Just one letter could have several dots and dashes! It was intimidating!

When I met Sam for the first time, I was nervous. Would I be able to communicate with him? With the mantra resounding in my head, "I'm here to help," I walked into his hospital room and introduced myself as "Janie, the volunteer doula." Immediately, Sam started frantically blinking, his way of letting us know he had something to say. Lucy, armed with paper and a pen started writing.

I immediately saw the confusion on her face, then, her brow furrowed, she asked Sam to slowly repeat the sentence. She methodically wrote out each letter "tapped out" through his eye movements. Finally, she turned to me and said sheepishly, "Sam says you have a gun."

Dumbfounded, I racked my brain, trying to come up with a reason that would make Sam think I had a gun! Clearly embarrassed by her husband's accusation, she said she must have misunderstood him. Just then, a nurse came in and announced it was time for Sam's bath.

I was still trying to figure this out as Lucy and I stepped into the hallway. Could it be Sam's medication? Maybe he mistook my new big iPhone for a handgun?? Then it hit me.

When I returned to Sam's room, I looked him in the eye, and with a big smile said, "'Janie's Got a Gun' by Aerosmith." With a twinkle in his eye, Sam nodded. Lucy burst out laughing. "Typical Sam," she said, "Always a jokester." I was in awe. This man, who was paralyzed and close to death, with sores all over his body, was still kidding around!

Over the next few months, this couple taught me what life is about. Lucy's unwavering love and dedication to her husband was beyond anything I had ever seen. She moved into the hospital room and became Sam's mouthpiece, tirelessly interpreting every word he blinked out for the nurses, aides, and doctors. She watched his breathing like a hawk, and monitored the BiPAP machine covering his mouth and nose. She barely got a full night's rest—Sam needed to be turned and adjusted constantly because he was in a tremendous amount of pain—yet Lucy soldiered on.

And Sam. Sam was the epitome of someone who lives life right up until his final breath. As doulas, we are taught to be silent and practice active listening. Because Sam couldn't speak, his eyes and facial expressions cued us in on his thoughts. His eyes would light up when he was happy. Darting his eyes back and forth, I could sense mischievousness. I could also tell when he was in pain, which was quite often. But the most heart-wrenching emotion for me was his gratefulness, which was evident after a guided meditation.

Guided imagery is one of the many tools we teach our doulas in order to relieve patients' physical and emotional pain. We bring them on a journey of the mind, taking them to a "special place" where they feel happiness and joy. For Sam, that was a hike through a beautiful wooded forest near his home. Keeping my voice soft, I instructed Sam to close his eyes, then took us on our hike. Through imagery, Sam was once again able to use his legs. I told him to feel how strong his body was, jogging along the lake, feeling the bright sunshine on his face and listening to the birds singing. Every sense in his body was alive within him. After twenty minutes of "travel," I looked over at Sam and saw tears were streaming down his face. For those few precious moments, he'd felt the joyous physical sensations of being able to use his body again.

I realized in that moment just how much Sam and Lucy had

given me. They taught me love, gratitude, appreciation. They taught me to live in the moment. That's such a cliché, but working with Sam and Lucy made that a reality for me.

As I continue to teach people to work with the dying, I remember all my patients. I remember the lessons each taught me; I remember their happiness and their heartache. I keep a journal by my bedside, recording the story of everyone I have had the honor to work with. Each one forever holds a place in my heart, keeping me on my path and imprinting their stories onto my soul.

ABOUT THE AUTHOR: Janie Rakow is cofounder and President of The International End of Life Doula Association (INELDA), a nonprofit organization dedicated to bringing deeper meaning and greater comfort to dying people and loved ones in the last days of life. Janie has been a hospice volunteer since 2001, and in 2015, she joined forces with end of life expert Henry Fersko-Weiss to start INELDA. Today, Janie, Henry, and their partner Jeri Glatter work tirelessly to bring greater awareness and understanding of doula work. Janie's work as a doula is complemented by her years of experience as a certified Emotional Freedom Technique (EFT) practitioner, hypnotherapist, and Reiki Level II practitioner.

Janie Rakow
International End of Life Doula Association (INELDA)
inelda.org
janie@inelda.org
facebook.com/inelda.org

How to Overwrite Memory
Amy Jayalakshmi Hellman

July 4th, 2017

Amy,

The next ten years of your life will be an exercise. Your re-education has already begun.

Nothing is accidental, you realize as you walk down Oxford's High Street, gazing across an unremarkable grey skyline of dreamy spires. Every moment is teaching you; when you forgive King for violently forcing you to choose life, you begin to heal all of this.

Two weeks after the attack, angered that your body panics when your nephews hug you, you decide to never let anyone ever steal your power again. This is profound, as owning your power means letting go of the unhealthy relationships in your life—and you have many. Realizing you do not yet possess the skills to sustain healthy boundaries with your family, you reclaim yourself by moving an ocean away. In a master's program at Oxford University, you study gender, identity, freedom, mythology, and romance languages. Very soon, you will have more ways to express your truth—and in four languages—the distance from your family helps you understand how feral you are—and how much work you still have to do to even begin to understand yourself.

Oxford conditionally accepts you for a PhD, only to reject you at the last minute, saying, "Your work is groundbreaking but not the sort of research we care to support." Your heart breaks, because the first man you let walk into your heart after King is about to move in with you that very day. You are both crushed.

Immediately following this, a kind Indian cabbie drives you home. He says, "My meter is broken—but I believe in Karma and everything happens for a reason—so let's agree on a fair fare beforehand."

Something is taking place that you simply are not aware of yet, so you listen and move to New York City.

Despite being close to your family again you feel lost and untethered, so you set severe boundaries to assert your independence. You rediscover yoga, completing three different teacher trainings, because intuitively you remember you came here to help others and you can only do that if you can handle yourself. You teach people about their bodies' potentials, and this helps you remember yours. This clarity and discipline fortifies you, reminding you that while being here can be painful, there are infinite ways to ease the suffering and extinguish it altogether. This allows you access to healthier relationships with your family.

New Year's, 2008

The night before the start of a master's program in education, something said *wait*. My family dynamic supplied an un-ending drama reel, which I felt responsible to heal: incidents involving the police, mental illness, miscommunications, stolen identities, rare physical diseases, botched surgeries, and crazy neighbors were all regular characters, themes, and storylines while I was growing up. I was an empath who did not know her own abilities or how to use them, and my family life was the best energy-sucking soap opera around. My addiction to their drama had made my own life unmanageable, and my attempts to process it for them had resulted in seven years of undergraduate study, three "nervous breakdowns", and multiple hospital visits. I also dealt with Irritable Bowel Syndrome, Bipolar disorder, major depression, impulsivity, eczema and anxiety, eating disorders, scoliosis, hernias, and a bone disorder whose name ironically abbreviated to OCD, not to mention untenable personal relationships replete with never-ending drama. I was tired and done. With everything.

The pull to end my life had been a close friend since early adolescence—my father was sick, I was a wheelchair-bound kid unable to fit in at school, and it had become clear to me that the world was full of suffering. Being intuitive, I was used to anticipating events before they happened. I was also plagued with the belief that I was not meant to live long. I wasn't afraid of dying, yet every time I felt that tug to "return home," something stopped me. Once, it was a cat named Buster, who sat with me all night. Once, it was my family, their never-ending reminder that I was needed. For as long as I could remember, I had stayed alive for others.

I am "loud." Whatever I focus on, I focus with purity of intention and "loudness," so the universe has absolute certainty what I'm up to. The failed suicide attempts, however, had lacked pure intention—they weren't "loud" enough. Perhaps if they were, God would pay attention and help move things along. What was the point of waiting here, suffering, when I could leave this world and be free? It was only when I finally showed up to my appointment with death that I would realize I'd changed my mind.

January 2008

I'd been blindly and stubbornly navigating a spiritual awakening for about five years when I met King. He washed dishes at the restaurant where I had been hired as a sous chef after deferring my master's program. King was proud, clever, and a liar; I knew it, but I was too tired to care. We shared a darkness; we were intuitive, powerful, and unskilled—a dangerous combination. Our connection was immediate, and before I knew it, we were dating, then living together. I was also paying all his expenses, including child support and a divorce attorney.

My family saw a man who in six weeks had isolated me from them and my friends, driven me into thousands of dollars of debt, and totaled my car. Their concern was justified, but I refused to end things. It wasn't about love; I didn't love him. It was proving to them that I had the freedom to choose my own life.

March 2008

In the fast lane heading south on I-95, King lit a cigarette and hit the rear of a Lincoln town car. Careening across three lanes, we narrowly missed three other cars before crashing against the Jersey barrier, causing me severe whiplash. Later that night, I replayed the accident; how had we survived that crash? How did we get off the highway safely? It was as if someone had said, *"NO. Not yet."* Apparently, I had more to do here.

June 2008

To pay off King's debt, I left the restaurant and took a position as an elementary and middle school Spanish teacher that upcoming August. I *felt* something was wrong, but years of judging my feelings for existing and being unable to discern myself from others had left me ill-equipped to protect myself against a sociopath. I felt his emotions—simple thoughts and lies—as my own, and did not know how to leave.

"Amy," he looked at me on the porch one afternoon, lit a Newport Light, and handed it over. "Let's get married."

I took the cigarette and inhaled deeply. The white plastic of my chair stuck to my thighs, the summer heat sweaty on my skin. My entire life—in all its possible futures—known and unknown, contracted before me in my inhalation.

"Okay," I exhaled smoke. *If this is my life,* I thought, *it will not last long.*

The night I returned from my best friend's wedding, King fell into a rage. Blaming me for his infidelities and failures, he choked on his words, as if wanting me to pull confessions from him. I played along, knowing exactly what to say and do to invite death. I yelled back at him. *It won't be long now,* the voices declared.

He threw me to the floor; my head hit the cabinets. Leaning against them, I hissed through a concussion, "If you ever touch me like that again, it is over."

But still I did not leave.

Fourth of July Weekend, 2008

On a night out, someone complimented my hoop earrings; I laughed and thanked them. As we drove home at 9:30, King, his breath stinking of beer, accused me of flirting.

By three a.m., our apartment was unrecognizable. Every picture, smashed. Fist-shaped holes covered the front door; broken Heineken bottles across the floor, he used one to corral me to the kitchen, where I sat holding myself as King held a ten-inch knife on me and listed every reason I should die. After three hours, I believed him. Then, a voice inside me said, *look at how much pain he has, Amy. This has nothing to do with you. Are you going to die for his pain?*

Suddenly, I understood that King's "truth" was nothing more than a death trap for me, expertly planned to appeal to my feral empathy, co-dependency, and addiction to drama. My death door had finally arrived. His emotions were not mine. I didn't want them to be. No matter the outcome that night, I finally understood that I was me and King was King.

He threw me down, pouring gallons of cold water on me, and dragged me by my hair across the glass-littered floor. It was then, after years of waiting for death, I chose, out loud, to live.

"Stop, please!" I pleaded, "I want to stay here!"

King, believing my exclamation was about our relationship, laid me on the bed and forced me, unsuccessfully, to have sex. I froze; he rolled away, there was a moment of quiet.

The part of me that clung to my choice got up, walked out the door and drove to my parents' house. Police, warrants, arrests, restraining orders, and court appearances followed.

I never saw King again.

Late August 2008

My reproductive organs flared with endometriosis, rupturing cysts, and yeast infections. Cystic acne exploded across my body; my digestion froze. Touch triggered panic attacks. With my parents' support, I recovered physically, but I still had no way of handling their anger, guilt, and fear, let alone my own.

King's contract with me made a final appearance that fall. As I drove to work, the used silver low-rider with tinted windows he'd picked out overheated. At the mechanic shop, I learned the car's history report was forged.

"You're lucky your car overheated," the mechanic said. "There's a poorly soldered pipe that could've exploded and killed you instantly if you hadn't stopped driving when you did."

Late August 2017

You change your karma by serving and teaching others; you see them, and they you. Your power returns to you incrementally, each layer reminding you of the dynamic balance needed between self-love and love of others. You remember the complex nature of human soul and physical form in balance and remind others. These students change your life, a continual reminder of why you chose life the morning after Independence Day. They teach you the cause and effect of kindness, laughter, and surrender.

Amy, your family respects and values your empathy; although it will take you years to accept the way they communicate this, you will forgive them—and yourself—for everyone's lack of fluency in the language of living. You will all learn how to encounter health, joy, and peace, and you will also watch them fail—like you have failed—and all of this is okay. They will value your advice and healing as you continue to grow, so keep growing, because your power is your choice. You finally feed yourself joyfully; through food, action, and thought, the parasites in your body and life leave, and you recover yourself. Let it happen.

One day, you will remember King, because he no longer haunts you, and neither does dying. You understand then how stubborn you were, and laugh about what happened, because it was the only way you knew then how to learn the lesson. You have so many more ways of learning available now.

Because you are brave, Amy, like a tonic, you will drink your fear over and over and watch it become love, surrounding yourself with life and a lifestyle that honors your choice to stay alive, your choice to remain here and thrive.

ABOUT THE AUTHOR: Amy J.'s journey as a teacher began over 20 years ago. Since then, she has had the pleasure of instructing individuals and groups of all ages and backgrounds in subjects ranging from academic to self-healing and more. Amy J. holds a master's degree from the University of Oxford and a master's and Certificate of Science from the ThetaHealing Institute of Knowledge. She uses her extensive background in academic instruction and the healing arts to guide those who are ready to more health, presence, and abundance in their lives.

Amy Jayalakshmi
Manna Healing with Amy J.
manna-healing.com
amy@manna-healing.com
706-804-2695

Getting to the Core of It
How I Discovered Power and Purpose in
One Extraordinary Moment
Christina Ammerman

The day I discovered my power was March 12, 2017.

That's not to say I was powerless up to that point. On the contrary, I had made some bold choices in my life, like quitting my IT career in 2004 to become a massage therapist, then starting my own business which evolved from a home-based practice into a brick-and-mortar healing center with a team of practitioners. I had also, in the face of open criticism, dared to believe in alternate healing methods and theories of life and the Universe—to speak of Angels and Ascended Masters as if they were my friends from down the block.

And, through my healing work, I had helped many other women find their power to make bold choices too. Despite all this, I still wrestled with a nagging feeling that I was circling a target but never quite hitting the bullseye. As much as I had accomplished, there were dreams that had gone unfulfilled. After eleven years my business wasn't yet as big as I imagined it would become. And though I was a very talented healer, I couldn't pin down exactly what I was supposed to do with those gifts and how to reach all the people I was intended to serve.

This was why I found myself sitting in a chilly ballroom of The Ritz Carlton, Atlanta, attending another David Neagle seminar. David had mentored many female entrepreneurs who went on to build internationally recognized brands—women like Ali Brown, Suzanne Evans, and Kendall Summerhawk—and I yearned for the breakthrough that would bring me to the same heights of success and service. After three years of his mentorship, though, I was still struggling to hit the bullseye...until that Sunday morning in March when he introduced a new topic: Core Wounds.

When he spoke those two words, my ears perked up, my breath caught, and I got the "spirit shivers."

"Listen up!" they said. "This is what you came here for. This is what you've been *waiting* for!"

What I learned that day about Core Wounds connected everything I'd been doing for the last eleven years. All the fumbling and stumbling in the dark, jumping from one fascination to the next—crystals, angels, Universal laws, spiritual ascension—and ditching each previous healing methodology for a new one I was learning now suddenly made sense.

The pain of my past also suddenly had a purpose. I immediately understood how the emotional and physical abuse I'd experienced as a child reinforced my Core Wound of "I am Unlovable," causing me to pull away from my peers throughout my school years and make few friends as an adult. I had lived much of my life alone.

But I saw the gift in my past, too! Feeling alone empowered me to seek my own path, because if, as I believed, people already didn't like me, then there was no need to limit myself to choices they would approve of.

As David spoke, I felt I was being given the missing piece to a cosmic puzzle. Among those pieces were my healing work and my commitment to the evolution of humanity. I already understood that the personal journey of each Lightworker is to reach a state of full God Consciousness in human form. And I understood the only thing holding us back is ourselves, in the form of limiting beliefs held in the subconscious mind.

I also practiced what I preached. Digging into my fears was how I had been able to keep my business going while most healers and coaches around me folded and went back to their day jobs. I'd been relentless in removing every obstacle I'd placed in front of myself, including the emotional scars of childhood, and yet the work remained frustratingly incomplete. I kept peeling the layers of the onion (my favorite metaphor for freeing the mind) but with no sense of when I would reach the center – if it was even possible. Now after years of searching I had in one moment discovered not only the center of the onion, but the tools to heal it, too!

I wasted no time in putting these ideas to the test. At the next break, when everyone else headed out for coffee and chitchat, I stayed firmly planted in my seat and gave myself a healing session, applying my belief-clearing technique to my "I am Unlovable" Core Wound.

Instantly, I felt a weight being lifted from me—a burden I hadn't even known I was carrying for forty-two years. I felt like I was breathing for the first time, and I'd swear the light in the room became brighter. I smiled like I had never smiled before. Was anyone watching me? For the first time ever, *I didn't care.* I felt happy and safe.

Meanwhile, unmistakable surges of spiritual energy ran through my body; I tingled all throughout my belly and hips as my lower chakras filled with the energy I'd been blocking all my life.

In the moments of that self-healing session, I came into my truest power – not only by healing my Core Wound, but by doing so, also uncovering my life purpose to help others do the same.

In the weeks and months that followed, I channeled additional information which further connected the dots—connections I couldn't see while my own Core Wound was active:

- The Core Wound happened to each of us while in the womb. Thus, while it's not something we were *created* with, it's something we were *born* with.
- It is always singular ("wound," not "wounds"), as it's the first wound to the psyche and energy field experienced in this life.
- The Core Wound is *not* inflicted by another. We chose it for ourselves, because the pure consciousness we incarnated as would not be compatible with Earth's dense energy.
- Now that Earth's and humanity's energies have evolved, we can survive as full Divine Consciousness—but to get back to that state, we must heal the Core Wound that originally brought us down from it. There is no way to bypass that step.

The Core Wound is expressed as one of two limiting beliefs, "I am Unworthy" or "I am Unlovable." At first it seemed odd that among seven billion people there would be only two possibilities; however, once I discerned how Core Wounds relate to our chakras (i.e., energy centers in the body), it all made sense.

Humans are designed to receive a constant flow of Divine Energy through exactly two portals: the Crown Chakra at the top of the head and the Root Chakra at the base of the spine. To make our energy compatible with Earth's, we had to cut off one of those sources; therefore, the wound could *only* be at the Crown Chakra or the Root Chakra. "I am Unlovable" —the Core Wound I had— is held in the Root Chakra. It cuts off the flow of Divine Feminine energy a person is intended to receive from the center of the Earth. Because that energy doesn't come into the Root Chakra, it also can't flow up through the Sacral or Solar Plexus Chakras into the Heart Chakra as designed, impacting relationships and personal power. The other Core Wound, "I am Unworthy," is held in the Crown Chakra. It cuts off the flow of Divine Masculine energy a person is intended to receive from the center of the Universe. Because that energy doesn't come into the Crown Chakra, it also can't flow down through the Third Eye or Throat Chakras into the Heart Chakra as designed, impacting intuition and expression.

Because the Core Wound cuts off one of the two intended flows of Divine Energy, we've been operating at 50% *at best!* This has led most people to also have the limiting belief, "I am Powerless." And, as we subconsciously sense the difference between our full potential and the level we're operating at, we try to compensate in other, unhealthy ways.

We struggle to gain dominion over our environment and look to others—spouses, families, government, religion—to provide because we don't recognize our power to do it for ourselves.

Now that I've healed my Core Wound and am not bound by its patterns, I can look back and clearly see the behaviors it was causing. Feeling unlovable meant that anytime someone showed me positive attention, I immediately latched onto them, whether or not they wanted a relationship, and whether or not that relationship was a healthy one. As bold as I was, I had a fear of rejection. It made me afraid to be wrong because then I would be criticized. That's why many of my big ideas never got started: if I couldn't foresee a successful ending I avoided the risk of beginning. I also did a great job of keeping my business "the best kept secret," because the more people who knew about it, the greater potential for rejection. I was unknowingly putting out a vibe that only "really safe" people would find me. Meanwhile, the Divine Feminine energies from my Root Chakra, which would have helped me feel supported in my endeavors, were cut off. I became a control freak, insisting on handling everything myself and further handicapping my business.

My Core Wound was the reason why, despite studying and teaching it for years, I hadn't gotten the Law of Attraction to work consistently for me. No matter how hard I had tried to make my "thoughts become things," I was simultaneously putting out a message of "the Universe doesn't support me," and so lack of support was what I often got. (By contrast, people with the Crown Chakra Core Wound "I am Unworthy" would be unlikely to believe in the Law of Attraction at all. Since the Crown Chakra holds our connection to Spirit/God/the Universe, people with that Core Wound are cut off from any inward experience of Spirit. Without that guidance they tend to go to one spiritual extreme or the other: either they're atheists, or they cling vehemently to religious doctrine. They also have an intense need to be right about things in general, rather than admit to themselves or anyone else that they don't have an inner confirmation of what's right or true.)

I know without question that healing our Core Wounds is the path to realizing our full power as human beings. In the first year since healing my Core Wound, my life has already changed in many wonderful ways. For instance, no longer burdened by shame of what I hadn't already done, I've made significant leaps in my business, including tripling the size of our practitioner team from two to six. To make room for them, I took a leap of faith and leased a second suite of offices.

I began healing others' Core Wounds—first with my private mentorship clients, then with groups so I could impact more people at a time. I branded my work "Fearless Freedom" and grew beyond my local brick-and-mortar business to an international scale.

Ironically, these amazing changes have as much to do with things I've *stopped* doing once I realized my power. I stopped trying to control everything and everyone. I stopped trying to earn love by working hard, and instead let the Universe support me by consciously seeking spiritual guidance for my everyday affairs. I stopped craving sugar and carbs because I now fill those voids with real joy and self-love. Most recently, I chose to separate from my husband of seventeen years, rather than continuing a relationship that didn't support my intentions for myself.

The biggest blessing by far has been the number of people I've connected with, now that I believe I'm a pretty awesome person to know and love. It's poetic that my forty-two-year journey of isolation took me to this destination, where I'm clearly meant to impact as many people as possible and help them heal their Core Wounds.

What was revealed in that ballroom on March 12, 2017 was my role in a widespread evolution of humanity. The more people who heal their Core Wound and find their Divine Power from within, the more that this planet will become a place of Love, Abundance, and Unity, without struggle or suffering.

I look forward to us living in that world together, my friend.

ABOUT THE AUTHOR: Christina Ammerman is a Master Energy Healer and Spiritual Mentor at Zenquility, a center for healing and higher consciousness in Gainesville, VA, of which she is also Founder and Director. Her passions include evolving human consciousness, Universal Law, and music; you can frequently find her singing with the overhead music in the local grocery store. Christina's calling is to connect with everyone who wishes to heal their Core Wound and embody Divine Love, Wisdom, and Power in their everyday life. To discover which Core Wound is holding you back from your true power, take the online quiz at CoreWoundQuiz.com.

Christina Ammerman
Core Wound Healer
ChristinaAmmerman.com
CoreWoundQuiz.com

A Lighter Soul
Transforming Grief into Gratitude
Angela Papay

My life is divided into periods: before June 11, 2011, and after. Before that day, I knew who I was. Wife and mother of two children, ages seven and five, and another on the way. Employee at an amazing company, with coworkers I thought of as family. Life wasn't perfect, but I never expected it to be. It was just my life, with its own cadence and direction, and I was doing my best to keep up with it all.

Then, June 11, 2011 happened.

My husband committed suicide, I became a widow, and the safe existence I had come to rely on crumbled around me.

I sleep-walked through my days, numb to everything and everyone, including my children. I looked around me, stunned that the world hadn't stopped turning. I put on a brave face and went through the motions, because if I stopped moving, I would die. When the initial shock wore off, darkness and fear and pain engulfed me. Even the smallest activities took every ounce of energy. Getting out of bed was a struggle; showering became optional.

Things only got worse after the baby was born, the little girl who would never meet her father. Darkness turned to panic, then a persistent sense of anxiety that plagued my every move. There I was, a thirty-two-year-old mother of three, asking friends to take me to the grocery because I was terrified to get behind the wheel of a car. I was convinced I would have a panic attack while driving and injure my children or someone else. I couldn't bear the thought of any more pain coming into my life. Even sleep provided no respite, as I had started having strange dreams about my husband.

I hunkered down in my house, measuring the days in nothing. I had nothing to look forward to, nothing—other than my children—to keep me going. But the cuddles never lasted long enough and their bedtime always came too soon. I would spend the rest of the night on the couch watching mindless television, exhausted yet afraid to close my eyes. When I did go out, I felt out of place. Seeing happy couples made me ache. I would make plans with people, then immediately want to cancel them. Oftentimes I did just that.

My wakeup call came in May 2012. By then I had a pretty high tolerance for anxiety, but after a twelve-hour panic attack I begged my best friend to take me to the ER. After a careful assessment, the medical staff decided to admit me. That decision would not only save my life, it would mark the beginning of my journey back into the light.

Once removed from the daily struggles of raising three kids by myself, I was forced to look at myself. I had to evaluate whether or not I was actively engaging in self-care (I definitely wasn't); if I was doing things I knew would make me feel better throughout the day (they never crossed my mind); and whether I actually wanted to feel better (I really, truly did). That evaluation led to self-discovery, which led to daily planning, which led to action, which led to progress.

At first, it seemed impossible. Who had time to journal and meditate and exercise? Certainly not a widowed mother of three. I considered it a good day if I had groceries in the house and got a chance to brush my teeth.

I started with slow, small baby steps. My first goal was to shower every day. It took me a while, but when I got to that point, I strove to make my bed every day. Then cook dinner a couple times a week, rather than living off cereal and pizza.

Soon those steps became noticeably larger. I started connecting with friends again. I resurrected old hobbies and picked up new ones. I left the house on a regular basis, no longer terrified of driving. I went back to being the mom I enjoyed being.

I was becoming me again.

Though I was making progress, my big breakthrough was still ahead. I can clearly remember that day—I was sitting on my couch, fighting off a panic attack. My parents had just left after an extended stay to help me with the kids, and now that they were gone I was left with those agonizing thoughts about all the things I was "supposed" to do and how I was "supposed" to live. I remember thinking about the day my husband died, finding his body and the chaos that ensued. Planning the funeral, with the seemingly hundreds of details that come with it, trying to bury the questions that I would never have the answers to and couldn't come to grips with. And then, out of the blue, a thought came to mind that made my eyes well up with tears.

I deserve more than this.

Now, there is one thing to know about me... Maybe it's my Catholic upbringing or just my constant fear of disappointment, but I rarely felt like I "deserved" anything. In fact, throughout my life, any time I asserted that I deserved something, it was immediately followed by an overwhelming sense of guilt and fear that I was being too selfish, had gone "too far." I bought cheap things, kept my head down, and put my dreams on the shelf. It wasn't that I thought I *didn't* deserve them, exactly; it was more like the thought that I did deserve them never crossed my mind.

The idea that I deserved more in life than sitting on my couch, trying to catch my breath was, at that time, foreign territory. I mulled it over for a bit and eventually the panic subsided. Then the kids needed something and I was off doing my daily routine again, the notion of deserving left somewhere on that couch.

But this strange thing started happening. The thought kept coming back. And it would hit me like a ton of bricks every time it did.

I deserve more.

How could I possibly want more? I have three, beautiful, healthy children. Isn't it selfish to want more?

I deserve more.

I had loving parents and good friends that had tried their best to help me through this horrible time. Should I just be grateful for them?

I deserve more.

I had a great job with an amazing company and worked with

people that I considered family.

Does wanting more make me one of those "entitled" people that tend to drive me crazy?

I deserve more.

Maybe I do!

This went on for weeks. And somewhere along the way, all the things I had started in the hospital (getting out of bed, brushing my teeth, showering) became routine again, and I started to feel a hunger inside I hadn't felt in a long time.

Slowly, I started seeking out new friendships (also foreign territory) and joined new groups. I opened up and started telling people my story. This was incredibly scary.

My husband committed suicide. What would these people think? That I couldn't keep him alive? That I wasn't enough? That I was a horrible wife? Would they think that suicide and widowhood are contagious?

But I kept telling the story because people asked. And the more I told it, the more people listened. They asked questions. They wanted to learn more.

I started meeting other widows, both in person and online, who needed someone to talk to. One of them was a family member. I went to see her the week of her husband's funeral and left seriously wondering if I had done more harm than good. But then she texted me and told me that talking to me was different, because she knew I understood what she was going through.

This struck a chord in me. After my husband died, what I wanted more than anything was to talk. My fellow widows got it in a way others didn't. I could say something that sounded completely insane, even in my head, and when I looked up, they would be nodding, relating, connecting. They validated what I was feeling, which was huge back then.

As I continued on my own healing journey, I started sharing what I had learned with other women. I started a Facebook group just for widows and reached out to grief centers in my local community, offering to talk to widows there. If I heard that someone I knew had become widowed, I went to the funeral or to their house and let them know I was available if they needed anything.

I explained that, for me, the painstaking—and often painful—process of re-emergence began with a single question:

Do I want to feel better?

This may seem like a no-brainer, however, many widows I spoke to seemed to cling to their sadness like a toddler clings to a blanket. It brings them comfort. It allows them to feel safe, because their sadness is familiar and comfortable to them. To be happy again invites the risk of being hurt and losing the happiness all over again. If you're always sad, there's no chance of being made sad… you're already there.

Several years ago, I heard a woman say, "If you want to feel good, do good." Now, this saying was becoming my truth and my mantra; eventually, it would become the inspiration for A Lighter Soul, my coaching practice geared specifically toward supporting and empowering widows.

Today, my goal is to reach as many widows as possible and help them understand that their lives are not over. In fact, they can live a life beyond their wildest dreams, even if they're grieving. Moving forward doesn't mean never looking back. They neither have to ignore their grief nor let it define them.

According to psychologists and sociologists around the world, losing a spouse is the most stressful event one can go through. I know this firsthand. My husband's death could have killed me. It could have driven me into a hole and never let me out again.

Instead, I've thrived. I've emerged. I've blossomed.

This year alone, I've done amazing things I didn't think I would ever be able to do. I joined CrossFit, despite a fair amount of trepidation. I got my nose pierced because I've always wanted to. I've traveled by myself for a conference attended by 14,000 other people. And, alongside fifteen teammates, I pulled a one-hundred-thousand-pound plane with a rope!

And I've fallen in love and I'm getting remarried.

At the time of this writing, I am eight days from my wedding. Without all the transformational work I've done, I never would have met my fiancée, let alone overcome my fear of being widowed again. The old me would have given into that fear and let myself drown in it.

But not the new me. When the fears bubbled to the surface, I wrote a post called "17 Days," in which I publicly called myself out. The outpouring of support—from widows and non-widows alike—was amazing. Most rewarding were the responses from other widows re-entering the dating world. My post helped them acknowledge and understand their own fears. Knowing you're afraid is knowledge. Knowing what you're afraid of is wisdom. Naming the fear is critical to overcoming it.

These days, I no longer sit on the couch and wonder what comes next; I picture what I want and I go after it. I will remarry, and will embrace the new life that is coming my way. This attitude has made me a better person, a better mom; moreover, it has made me better equipped to help other widows who want to do the same thing.

Life is good. Life is hard. Life is beautiful. And I want it all.

ABOUT THE AUTHOR: Angela Papay knows firsthand how hard it is to recover from catastrophic loss. Widowed during her third pregnancy, she struggled to care for her children while battling depression and anxiety. Her journey to wellness taught her the power of connectedness and inspired her to use her own experiences to help others. To this end, she translated those experiences into practical, empowering lessons, which she shares through her website, ALighterSoul.com. As a Robbins-Madanes Certified life and resilience coach, she helps women discover their inner power for overcoming grief, heartache, and self-destructive behaviors. Angela is newly remarried and lives in Ohio with her husband and their five children.

Angela Papay
A Lighter Soul
alightersoul.com
angela@alightersoul.com
330-714-2758

Finding My Inner Compass
Michelle Giliberto

The Pineapple and the Pendulum

"Pineapple is safe for her to eat." I looked at the weight in my hand, heavy as a brick. Complete stillness. I felt my chest constrict. For just a moment, I could feel my body tighten. The kind of feeling you get when you sense impending danger. I looked down at the shiny silver chain in my hand. So pretty, with its delicately carved bob on the end. I was holding a pendulum, a tool with which I was learning to dowse, or derive information from. It was actually one of several forms of energy testing I was studying.

The pendulum was completely still in my hand and I could hear in my head a loud "No!" What followed from that moment was a mixture of emotions and the next phase in an epic journey of empowerment for me.

You see, I had begun learning energy testing because I wanted to understand how to extract information from within. Actually, it was more of a need than a want. My young daughter was very sick, and she was getting worse. She had been subjected to every type of test but doctors couldn't get to the core of the problem. She seemed to react to all kinds of household products, weather, vitamins, and foods. She had constant ear infections and frighteningly high fevers most of the time. We were at the doctor's office every week.

Desperate to help her, I prayed for guidance, yet night after night I found myself helplessly holding my feverish little one.

It was at the point of my deepest sorrow and fear that the Universe delivered not one but two angels in human form. One, a shamanic healer, taught me how to use the pendulum. She explained how to understand my individualized answers: if the pendulum remained completely still it was a "no" and if it began to swing back and forth, it was a "yes."

The other, a homotoxicologist, showed me how to muscle test using my own body. Initially I was skeptical that this was useful— or even real! Learning the science of how certain neuropeptides work with our muscles to deliver answers helped, as did the accurate information we received time and time again. It was like an art form and a miracle, all in one.

I wanted to be able to do it myself, except I didn't see myself as an "artist." After all, I hadn't gone through the initiations that my healer friend had and I didn't have a Ph.D. like the homotoxicologist. When the healer said, "You will use this one day to help many others," I really couldn't fathom it. I didn't doubt her dowsing ability, only my own. I told myself I was just exploring out of curiosity.

Still, I practiced, asking silly things I already knew, like what color my PJs were or what I had eaten that day. At first it was pretty exciting to see a yes when I asked if I'd had grapefruit for breakfast when in fact I had. Then I got adventurous, asking questions I didn't yet know the answer to—real, breaking-news type questions like, will peaches be on sale today? Or, do I have enough diapers in the house to last the week? I got pretty jazzed up when I dowsed a yes to the peaches question, only to go to the supermarket and see that they were thirty cents less than usual. I could plan on making peach cobbler before even going to the store! As you can probably tell, I wasn't yet ready to ask the tough questions!

So I kept asking the silly ones, sometimes using the pendulum and sometimes using muscle testing. At that time I was mainly using the O-ring method, by interlocking my fingers in two rings and tugging to see if they stayed connected. If they did it was a "yes" and if they came apart it was a "no." Every time I did it, I noticed what my body felt like. When the answer was "yes" I noticed an expansive feeling, like my chest was opening, and my breathing became easier. When I got a "no" I would feel that tight constriction in my chest. Each time I used it, I could see the pendulum or my fingers "show" me the answer while simultaneously feeling the corresponding sensations in my body. I was hooked. In time, I began to understand that energy testing, in its various forms, offered an opportunity to make the intangible, tangible.

Yet I was still not ready to ask questions that would impact my decision-making around my daughter's health. Instead, I made lists of the important questions for my next appointment. Then it dawned on me that I was answering trivial questions within seconds and making myself wait, sometimes for weeks, for crucial, potentially life-changing information. Then I got a much-needed nudge from the Universe, when I fed my daughter pineapple.

Within minutes, I watched her change before my eyes. Her breathing was heavier, her eyes got hollow and she became really agitated. This happened a lot—usually with new things—and it was becoming difficult to keep up with the triggers. I would then run through a litany of questions in my mind—what did I do differently today? Was it something she ate? Drank? Breathed in? *What is it?!?* I thought about the pineapple, then jotted it down to bring to one of the pros, except no one was available. My angels were busy.

Waiting may seem like no big deal, except that she was reacting to more foods all the time. I had already eliminated so many things she loved to eat, I didn't want to take away another—especially one that was otherwise nutritious—unless I was sure. I imagined a life in which she got to eat healthy food of her choosing, and I didn't have to worry about their effect on her.

It was the proverbial moment of truth. Out came my pendulum and I tested her relationship to pineapple several different ways, all with the same answer. Pineapple was not safe for her to eat at the moment. The feeling in my body and the answers all matched. Later, testing by my two angels yielded the same information. Sure enough, when she didn't eat pineapple, my daughter's symptoms calmed. (How we worked through the layers to get to the core issue is a story for another time.)

Bolstered by this validation, I started practicing with those important questions, though I tested it many, many times before I felt comfortable doing it without backup from my angels.

My testing matched the results of the scientific tests; in fact, energy testing was often able to go beyond what those tests were capable of showing. Sharing this information with our physician then helped her order more precise tests. We were going deeper and getting answers that helped my daughter heal. As I saw her become more vibrant and healthy, I felt more confident in my ability to access the infinite information that already resided within me and her.

As I write this, she is currently a healthy tween, empowered to do her own energy testing, which shows her she can happily enjoy pineapple and many other goodies.

But this is really only the beginning of my story, the tiniest tip of the iceberg.

Analysis Paralysis

The information about the pineapple did facilitate my daughter's healing; however, several questions remained. *Why* was pineapple hurting her? What else was causing her symptoms? How do I help her get to the bottom of this?

Then there was my son, who had been diagnosed with Autism Spectrum Disorder. His symptoms were varied and extreme, and trying to figure them out was like trying to put together the pieces of the most intricate puzzle you can imagine.

Was it genetic? From me? From his father? Was it the antibiotic I took while pregnant? Was it the medical intervention he endured right after he was born? Was it something he ate? Toxins in the environment? Vaccines? Karma? If I'd eaten 100% organic, meditated every day, and never got stressed during my pregnancy would he have been okay? WAS IT ALL MY FAULT?

Each day I had to figure out what was safe and best for him. Which practitioners were a good match; did he need speech therapy; auditory processing therapy; ABA therapy? Will this or that medical test give us more information? Which supplements are beneficial and not harmful? What can he tolerate today?

Between the questions about my children's health challenges and those about other life situations, I often felt like I was going down a rabbit hole. For every answer I got it seemed I had ten more questions, and it was causing more anxiety. I realized that I was asking most of my questions out of panic and fear.

What once had me feeling empowered now felt like I was juggling with one too many balls in the air. The art of the question had been consumed by my fear around the challenges I faced. Exhausted and overwhelmed, I hit a wall I call analysis paralysis. I don't think it has to be this way for everyone, but I now realize I had to hit that wall in order to go beyond my fear and anxiety.

One day, at the end of my rope, I surrendered. I literally went down on my knees, crying and asking the Universe WHY? Why was my life like this? Why were my kids suffering? Why was I suffering? Did it have to be like this? I didn't want to do it like this anymore. I needed a change. I closed my eyes and saw myself rise up above my body, like I was looking into a picture of my whole life from the outside.

From this vantage point I could see all the suffering, but I could also see all my progress—from asking the silly questions to those that helped my kids. I had also found some pretty awesome answers for my own health and received positive feedback from friends who had benefitted from my energy testing skills. Seeing all this made me feel a little better.

When I told my healer friend about this experience, she promptly reminded me of her long-ago prediction that I would help others. She asked me to pay attention to my feelings and start creating my life from my heart's desires. Wait, somehow I'd helped create all that suffering? That was a bitter pill at first, but then a lightbulb went off. If that was true, it also meant I'd helped create all that learning and healing too. If I had a hand in creating life to be that hard, then couldn't I create it to be amazing? It was a truly liberating thought.

I came to understand that living our experience facilitates our soul's expansion. Part of my mission in this life is to feel free and empowered and, through example, share that experience with others so that they may know it is possible. And from this perspective, I began to create my life differently.

I still have stressful moments, but that stress now feels like a red ribbon tied on my finger. It reminds me to step outside the chaos and ask: "What am I creating here? What am I learning? How would I like to feel?" Immediately, I am moved from fear to empowerment.

These questions, paired with energy testing, have helped me create a life in which I feel centered, connected, and joyful—with two healthy kids to boot.

One of my greatest joys, however, has been witnessing my clients step into their own power. We all have what we need within; we just need the right tools to bring them to the surface.

ABOUT THE AUTHOR: Michelle Giliberto is a passionate, intuitive healer who uses her extensive knowledge of Metaphysical Anatomy, Dowsing, and Energy Kinesiology to facilitate physical, mental, emotional, and spiritual transformation. After twelve years in the corporate world, Michelle embarked on a journey to help her children heal from chronic illness. She also co-founded Epidemic Answers, a non-profit organization that connects parents and caregivers of compromised children with recovery solutions. Today, she operates Healers Who Share, a company that produces quantum healing formulas and offers empowering educational seminars. Michelle, who is also a Reiki Master and Theta Healer, serves clients in person and remotely throughout the United States, Canada, and Europe.

Michelle Giliberto
Healers Who Share, LLC
MichelleGiliberto.com
HealersWhoShare.com
info@michellegiliberto.com

From Revenge to Soul Restitution

LeNae Goolsby, JD

Man's extremity is God's opportunity. ~ *2 Timothy 4:16-18*

It was the end of another bleak and dreary day. Another day I had managed to survive. I grabbed my reward—a twelve-dollar bottle of Chardonnay—and plopped down on the dirty cream velour sofa, planning to drown the depression, stress, and anger roiling within me.

I reached for the television remote, vaguely pleased to find that *Revenge*, one of a handful of superficial shows I kept up with, was on. It was then, as I sat there, eyes glued to the screen like a mindless disciple, when it occurred to me that I was not watching this cheesy nighttime soap for entertainment purposes; I was using it to fuel my own ideations of vengeance.

Let me back up a bit.

Like many women, I wear many hats. I have also, over the course of my life, had a litany of completely unrelated and sometimes quirky jobs.

Right out of high school, I worked in a book distribution warehouse. I also clocked time in a bra distribution factory, twisting bra straps around hooks on tiny plastic hangers; answered phones for a Chattanooga construction company; and handled various administrative tasks for a Nashville-based non-profit organization focused on epilepsy. I even played Girl Friday to various arrogant, if not disillusioned, power-seeking men, from a podiatrist to the rich and famous to slick-talking lawyers and insurance brokers.

Prior to marriage, I served as a paralegal and law office administrator for a couple of Orlando, Florida's most high-maintenance solo practitioners. Needless to say, I learned how to manage issues and…how to solve problems. I felt like I was kind of like a law-abiding version of Fran Moore from the 2001 Gene Hackman film, The Heist. "I'm the go-getter," Fran famously quipped, "You tell me what you want me to go get."

When I married my husband, Trip, I would not only take on the role of wife, but also "Medical Practice Administrator" for his private community oncology and hematology practice. I'll never forget the day my step-father-in-law and Trip's administrator, learned we were finally getting married after five long years of dating. He walked up to me carrying what seemed to be a five-foot stack of white, three-ring binders and dumped them in my arms, essentially saying, "Good luck, I'm out." And back to Upstate New York he went, leaving me standing there with a bundle of binders and a confused, freaked-out look on my face.

It took about year (or so) of me leaning on, "I'm sorry, I'm new here" to figure out the intricacies and nuances of managing and marketing a multi-million-dollar cancer clinic. But God as my witness (in my best Scarlett O'Hara voice) I did.

Oddly enough, once things calmed down, I found myself unsettled, unchallenged, bored. I'd always wanted to be a lawyer; or rather, I always wanted to overcome my fear of lawyers (a totally different story). Before I knew it, I was knee-deep in law school applications, then beginning my "1L" (first year of law school) at a little-known private school in the Appalachian Mountains. As I was also now the mother of a nine-month-old, that first year was a stress-filled blur of steep learning curves and deadlines, but again that is a whole other story.

Suffice it to say, I survived that first year, then transferred to Tulane in New Orleans, because (a) I was accepted, and (b) I'd finally convinced Trip to join a "team" of physicians that could support and help manage him. After a year of nationwide interviewing, he had accepted an offer with a physician-owned multi-specialty clinic in an up and coming town in Louisiana.

My intention, post-graduation, was to hang a wooden shingle with my name richly engraved in some fancy Charles Dickens-esque font and start my commercial litigation practice. It never occurred to me that I would never, or at least not to date, practice law. I mean, that private university tuition was a six-figure education.

I used to tell people that I was derailed from pursuing practice through a series of cataclysmic events. But I now understand that life doesn't happen to me, life happens for me. And the life that is happening for me does so because consciously, or unconsciously, as the case may be, I create it. But I did not realize this in 2011, and so when shortly after my graduation Trip once again asked for my help, I put my dreams of shingle-hanging aside and once again donned my medical hat.

His practice, our family's livelihood, had been devastated by a perfect storm of local medical community politics and exacerbated by national healthcare politics, the crisis in pharmaceutical costs and acquisitions, and the ever-deepening Medicare cuts (a/k/a "sequestration") to physician reimbursement. Almost overnight we found ourselves hundreds of thousands of dollars in debt and unable to meet our personal financial obligations, much less afford the chemotherapy drugs needed to continue providing care to our patients.

Eight days before Christmas 2011, my world tanked, along with any sense of security. My emotions quickly escalated from shock, to depression, to anger. In my anger, I narrowed my focus to a couple of local individuals as the culprits "responsible" for my family's financial crisis—never mind all the other antagonists. Mentally I became fixated on getting back at the people within arm's reach, so to speak, who I believed threatened my marriage, ruined my financial security and peace of mind, and robbed me of my joy.

It was in the midst of this "storm" that I found myself watching that fateful episode of *Revenge*. Ironically, it was then, as I worked on that bottle of Chardonnay, that I experienced perhaps the greatest moment of clarity in my life. As much as I despised the hateful people for what they had done to me and my family, I could not hurt them without hurting myself. Even my legal mind could find no karmic loophole for what I was envisioning. And with that, I turned off the TV and never watched (or plotted) Revenge again.

Even at the low point, I at least knew that when one goes to dig a ditch for another person, he/she may as well dig two. We cannot take someone else down without also taking ourselves down (thank you, Confucius!).

So I stopped obsessing about my "enemies" and instead made a one-hundred-eighty-degree turnaround. The spiritual quest that followed led me to many brilliant teachers, including Dr. Wayne Dyer. One quote popularized by Dyer deeply resonated with me: *"We are not physical beings having a spiritual experience; we are spiritual beings having a physical experience."*

The concept wasn't exactly new to me—as a child I'd heard some version of it in church—but it had gotten lost in the hustle and bustle of my life. Now, for the first time, I really thought about it. If we are infinite spiritual beings having a physical experience, then all my drama and trauma, while significant in the moment, was, in the scheme of things, just a blip on the screen, a minor hiccup, a pebble in my shoe, easily removed with the right tools.

From here, I delved deeper into the works of Dr. Dyer, as well as Louise Hay, Eckhart Tolle, Dr. Eben Alexander, Anita Moorjani, and others. Over time, my perspective on all of my past experiences shifted and clarity, inner peace, and forgiveness replaced depression, stress, anger, and that unhinged desire for revenge.

While it was not easy by any means, Trip and I kept our practice afloat through 2011 and 2012. And, at the end of 2013, we successfully transitioned The Oncology & Hematology Institute of Southwest Louisiana into what is known today as Infinite Health Integrative Medicine Center.

This new venture provides empowering motivational medicine for the body, mind, and soul via our proprietary Four Pillar Approach to optimized health and longevity. Men and women from all over (even as far away as Chile) seek us out when they are ready for more than what traditional reactive medicine has to offer. Our patient-partners are achieving amazing transformational results, and we are impacting lives that would have never otherwise been reached had we not gone through the fire, so to speak.

In my limited, revenge-fueled spiral, I could have never conceived how that devastating day in 2011 could be the catalytic change required for the thriving, life-empowering, and fun medical practice we have today.

While continuing to fulfill my role as Practice Administrator for Infinite Health, I worked to develop my own intuitive abilities. In 2013, after completing training in a universal laws-based spiritual and life-coaching program, I finally got to hang my shingle, not as an attorney, but as an intuitive empowerment life coach.

Today, my professional life is all about creating those same joyful, transformational shifts in my clients. I help them realize that they too are the creators of their life experience. They move from subconscious self-sabotage to become deliberate intenders and conscious creators. We work together to identify areas where their power has been abdicated and how they can reclaim it. We observe what no longer serves and clear it in order to create the space for that which brings them closer to alignment with their bliss.

I still wear many hats—wife, mother, coach, author, and speaker—all of them incredibly fulfilling. Even after all this time, I find myself amazed at how I went from that hurt, angry, victimized, depressed woman to one who has become a source of light for others. All it took was that one coherent choice to move out of the darkness—and the same could be true for you.

ABOUT THE AUTHOR: LeNae Goolsby is a personal power activator, intuitive soul coach, and author of numerous globally syndicated articles and two books thus far. She is a leader in the business of integrative medicine and is the practice administrator for Louisiana's premier integrative provider, Infinite Health Integrative Medicine Center. LeNae holds a Juris Doctor from Tulane and a certificate from the Duke University Integrative Medicine Center Leadership Development Program. When she's not somewhere on the I-10, LeNae is keeping up with her three children, affectionately known as IV, Huck and L-Belle.

LeNae Goolsby
Personal Power Activator, Author, Speaker & Soul Coach
LeNaeGoolsby.com
lenae.goolsby@gmail.com
@URWorthTheLove

Reborn:
Empowerment Through Faith and Forgiveness
Michelle Dillard

On our journey through life, we all have many teachers. Some teach with love and compassion, while others present us with challenges that we must overcome in order to grow. I can honestly say that of all my teachers, none has been more powerful than my mother. My mother was born and raised in North Carolina at a time when, though slavery was no longer in existence, there was a great deal of racism. It was both overt and insidious, affecting not only relations between whites and blacks but those within the black community. Back then, the lighter one's skin, the better, and my mother, who was brown-skinned, would only date very light-skinned men. My father was light-skinned, as I am, yet I still didn't quite fit my mother's ideal image of what I should look. As a child I remember her comparing me to my Caucasian girlfriends and finding my lips were too big, my nose and derriere too large. I didn't measure up in other ways as well, and she never passed up an opportunity to let me know it, usually by calling me stupid. It wasn't the only derogatory name she used, but it was the most painful. It was also confusing; for the life of me, I simply could not understand why a parent would say such things to their child.

Despite her treatment of me, my mother, like most parents, wanted me to surpass her in education and in life. Well, I did both. Growing up I was an athlete, played two musical instruments, took ballet and tap dancing, and was a figure skater for fourteen years. I was also a good student and received my master's degree from an Ivy League university. I was very competent in all that I did, yet my mother continued to devalue me. She called me stupid so much that I began to believe that I actually was.

Over time, the "seeds" my mother planted took root and grew in my mind. My self-image was damaged, my self-esteem was almost non-existent, and I had a great deal of self-doubt; all had serious repercussions in my life. I was sexually promiscuous and sometimes unsafe, resulting in three abortions. In college, I smoked marijuana and drank, and placed myself in very risky situations. I also became involved with men who cheated on me and otherwise disrespected me; some were verbally and even physically abusive. I thought it was my fault that they treated me the way they did. I felt I deserved the poor treatment.

My low self-esteem extended to my career as well. Over the years I let many opportunities in the workplace slip by me because a voice inside my head told me I wasn't good enough or capable enough. These lies I had been told throughout my life made it impossible to know who I was or realize my worth as a human being. It very nearly led to the destruction of my soul and psyche.

That's where my other powerful teacher—God—stepped in. Giving my life to Jesus happened in what I believe to be a supernatural way, orchestrated by God. One night, I fell asleep with my television tuned to one channel and woke up with it on a completely different one: the Christian Broadcasting Network. Dr. Charles Stanley, pastor of the First Baptist Church in Atlanta and founder of Touch Ministries, was speaking about salvation, sin, and death. It wasn't a fire and brimstone kind of message but it definitely lit a fire in me. After hearing Dr. Stanley's message, I made the decision right then and there that I wanted to give my life to Jesus and accept Him as my savior.

I have been a Christian since 2014, and it has completely remade my life. It hasn't always been an easy journey. I thought once I became a Christian that most, if not all of my problems, would disappear. In fact, my life became more difficult because now I had to walk that Narrow Path—I had to live my life differently, think differently, treat others differently, and the most difficult, I had to FORGIVE even those who I felt didn't deserve forgiveness.

I also had to die to my old self and be reborn. But what did this really mean? From the beginning, I had heard that being a Christian means "I am a child of the Most High God," and although I accepted those words at face value, I didn't really understand their significance. Then, one day, like a miracle, it really hit home. Being a child of the Most High God means, amongst other things:

I am Forgiven – I am Loved – I am Redeemed – I am Delivered – I am Blessed – I am Healed – I am Valuable and I am Worthy. I am GOD'S MASTERPIECE.

What a wonderful feeling to know who exactly I am. I am not defined by my mother, my supervisor, my friends, or my co-workers, but by the Most High God. He is my Creator, He is my Father and I am His child. God loved me yesterday, loves me today, and loves me tomorrow. His love is not based on my appearance or my abilities but on the fact that I am His creation—I am His child. His love is like no other. Knowing these things has changed my life and the way in which I see myself. I know now that I am valuable, I am worthy, I am loved.

With God's help, I also began to see my mother from a different perspective. I could have easily hated her for the things that she said to me, and, for a while I believe I did. As I grew spiritually, I came to see her as the wounded and damaged person she is. Is she this way because of her upbringing in the South? Is it because she was physically and verbally abused by her first husband? I believe that it is a combination of both and possibly some other things that I have no knowledge of. What I do know is that for whatever reason my mother doesn't like herself—she doesn't like being an African American and all that goes along with that. I have been—and still am—a source of shame for her and a target for her anger and self-hatred because of my physical appearance. I am a reminder of who she is.

My mother is now ninety years old and has dementia. I am her primary caregiver. I have given up the life I knew to take care of her. That life may not have been much, but it was mine. I gave up an apartment, my sanity, solitude, spontaneity, freedom, and my cat Coco. There have been times when I felt isolated, almost like I was the only person on earth dealing with a situation like this.

Moving into my mother's home—into her space—made me feel ten years old again. All the anger, resentment, and hurt flooded back and I began to feel powerless and weak. No matter how I feel and what derogatory name I am called, I still have to take care of her. Many who don't know my mother have told me it's the disease. Yes, that is partly true but I also know that a great deal of her old behavior pattern is being *magnified* by the disease. Funny how life goes, isn't it? As difficult as it is, I know that God has put me in this situation to teach me how to forgive. Yes, my mother still calls me stupid and sometimes it still hurts, but only when I forget who I really am and who defines me. I believe that forgiveness is one of the things that a lot of Christians deal with— it is sometimes difficult to forgive someone who we may feel doesn't deserve it. But as God forgave me for my shortcomings, I must learn to forgive others. I haven't always liked my mother, but I will always love her, and I am forever grateful that she wanted me to fly higher than she could in her life. At the same time, I need to continue to forgive her so that I am no longer a prisoner of the pain or under the control of my emotions. Most importantly, I need to forgive her so that I can heal. I have let my mother know that I forgive her for some things—I am still working on the others and God is working on me. He knows me and He is patient with me.

At fifty-six years old, I no longer recognize the insecure, wounded person I used to be. I have more confidence, I am more of a risk-taker (being part of this wonderful project is proof of that), I am humble in my abilities but I have a can-do unstoppable attitude. I also no longer tolerate certain things or people in my life because I know my worth and value as a human being.

My story is about my journey to self-love, self-awareness, and forgiveness. The main characters are myself and my mother, but the true author is God. He is my Creator and my best friend, and He has always been there whenever I felt alone, abandoned, rejected, and unloved. Even when I wasn't paying attention to Him, He still loved me and was there for me. Even today, he continues to heal and deliver me, and I know He will do so right up to the minute He calls me home.

Whenever I am having a hard time letting go of the past or find myself worrying about the future, I remember that He is still working on me, and He is still working on you too. You need only open the door to your heart and let Him in.

ABOUT THE AUTHOR: Michelle Dillard is a Certified Professional and Stress Management Coach passionate about helping her clients become the best version of themselves. She holds a master's degree in Social Work from Columbia University in New York and a master's degree in Guidance & Counseling from Long Island University, also in New York. In the past she has worked with abused children, substance abusers, and parolees. Inspired by her own life experiences, she seeks to assist others suffering from poor self-esteem realize their inherent worth and value as human beings and make emotionally healthy choices in all areas of their lives.

Michelle Dillard
Dawning Light Coaching
dawninglightcoaching.com
michelle@dawninglightcoaching.com
302-507-7898

Co-Creating Wonderland
Kathy Sipple

"When you have to turn into a chrysalis—you will someday, you know—and then after that into a butterfly, I should think you'll feel it a little queer, won't you?" ~ Lewis Carroll, Alice's Adventures in Wonderland

It's 1978 and my sixth-grade class in Virginia Beach, Virginia is putting on a musical, *Alice in Wonderland*. Shy, and a new student at school, I do not try out for a role, instead resigning myself to a member of the Flower Chorus.

During rehearsals I stand on the sidelines, watching and listening to my classmates recite their lines and speaking them silently to myself to pass the time. On opening day, the girl playing the Dodo bird gets the flu and is unable to perform. Because I know the lines (and the costume fits), I am chosen to replace her.

It is exhilarating to dance and sing onstage, all the better to do so behind the masked anonymity of the large beak I wear as part of my costume. And, since I am a last-minute addition to the cast, my name doesn't appear in the printed playbill either. Though no one is likely to know, or remember, my involvement, I am proud to help "the show go on" and prove to myself I am capable of more than I realize.

For the next thirty years, I manage to avoid appearing before a large audience.

Down the Rabbit Hole

"But I don't want to go among mad people," Alice remarked.
"Oh, you can't help that," said the Cat, "We're all mad here. I'm mad. You're mad."
"How do you know I'm mad?" said Alice.
"You must be," said the Cat, "or you wouldn't have come here." ~ Lewis Carroll, Alice's Adventures in Wonderland

It's October 2008 and my sister has awakened from a month-long coma after suffering a brain injury. She remains hospitalized at the Rehabilitation Institute of Michigan in Detroit where she works valiantly toward recovery despite many challenges, including financial pressures. My husband and I have come from our home in Valparaiso, Indiana to lend support.

I take on the role of "communications manager," creating a patient blog to keep friends and family updated on her progress. Hospital staff, along with many others, begin to subscribe and soon the number of supporters grows to over 500, assisted in large part by social media. Through my communications, I get to know some of my sister's creative, free-spirited friends. Among them are musicians who want to help with her mounting expenses. Each year, they play at a ball— "DEB," they call it—and choose a cause for which they raise funds during the event. I'm very moved when they tell me they have chosen my sister as this year's beneficiary. They also invite me to speak at the DEB, which is happening in a few weeks. Grateful for the help and despite my lifelong discomfort around speaking in public, I agree immediately.

Unfamiliar with the event, I Google it. Oh my God! I realize I have just agreed to speak at the Detroit Erotica Ball (DEB)! Just glimpsing some of the online photos from the previous year makes me blush. I recall the traditional advice given to nervous public speakers: imagine the audience in their underwear... Well, let's just say that in this case, no imagination was necessary.

On the night of the ball, I rely on a bit of liquid courage to get onstage and face my audience, which is over 2,000 strong. Somehow I get through it and though we don't raise much money toward my sister's cause, the experience is invaluable. Like my childhood performance of the Dodo, it reminds me that I am capable of more than I know, especially when rising to a challenge to help someone else.

Through the Looking Glass

It's January 2009. My sister is finally released from the hospital and my husband and I head home to Indiana. Much has changed in the six months we were away, including the mortgage crisis—now in full force as one large bank after another declares bankruptcy.

We are realtors, and between our extended absence and the challenging financial climate, the handwriting is on the wall. A new course of action is required, but what?

I apply for jobs, but none materialize. As I wait, I begin to wonder if the communication tools and methods we had used to build community for my sister's health crisis could be adapted for business and nonprofit marketing. But would it work? The media is now calling what we're in The Great Recession, and many small businesses are struggling.

I summon my courage and begin knocking on doors. I propose my idea to the Executive Director at a local business incubator. "So you would teach workshops on social media marketing then?" she asked reasonably. As silly as it sounds, I hadn't considered the method of delivery before this moment. "Yes, of course," I reply, with no idea of what is required since I had never taught a class before and social media marketing is new to nearly everyone, myself included.

I gather case studies, build slide decks, and lesson plans. The first workshop sells out and feedback is quite positive. I continue offering workshops and talks to various business groups and local universities, fueled by a desire to empower people to learn tools that can help them build an online brand. I don't think much about my own brand, I just keep moving.

Cat: Where are you going?
Alice: Which way should I go?
Cat: That depends on where you are going.
Alice: I don't know.
Cat: Then it doesn't matter which way you go.
~Lewis Carroll, Alice's Adventures in Wonderland

At the end of 2009 I win an award naming me Indiana's most influential woman in social media. In an interview, I am asked, "What's next?" I stammer an answer, but realize I don't know. Now that I have taught many the skills they need to do their own marketing, what else is needed from me? I sign up for a vision board workshop the next month, hoping for guidance.

My completed board includes many images of the earth, trees, vegetables, and people exercising outdoors, which is somewhat surprising since my work does not involve any of these in a meaningful way. I also clipped a headline reading "Prophet Motive: Building a Platform for Social Change" and pasted it on, with no idea what it meant. I reflect on the vision repeatedly over the next year, and though it doesn't provide a road map per se, it offers me clues.

My husband and I buy a state park pass and begin hiking with our dog. During our walks, we sometimes spot interesting plants or animals and also meet naturalists who share their knowledge of the local ecosystem with us. I find myself wishing there was a way for others to learn about this.

One day during a walk in the woods it occurs to me that a podcast could be a platform for social change! I schedule various guests and name my show 219 GreenConnect— "219" is our area code in Northwest Indiana; "green" refers to sustainable and "connect" because I intend to connect people to one another and to new and fresh ideas about the environment.

Interviewing people is easy for me. It doesn't feel like public speaking at all, as I am completely absorbed and interested in my guests' stories. It's not about me, I am merely the facilitator. Dozens of episodes and several years later, I receive an email:

You are selected to receive a Conscious Evolutionaries Chicagoland "Golden Innovator Award" to honor your contributions towards co-creating a better world through your 219 GreenConnect podcast. This prestigious award will be presented to you in person by Barbara Marx Hubbard, the founder of The Foundation for Conscious Evolution.

A futurist and author of several books, including one of my favorites, Conscious Evolution: Awakening the Power of Our Social Potential, Barbara has been a hero of mine for over a decade. Barbara believes millions of us are moving into a "social chrysalis," evolving culture toward a new type of society, relying on our imaginal cells to help us express our unique creative gifts, offered for integration into the body of the societal butterfly none of us has seen yet and is now evolving.

"Who are you?" said the Caterpillar.
Alice replied, rather shyly, "I — I hardly know, sir, just at present —at least I know who I WAS when I got up this

morning, but I think I must have been changed several times
since then."
"What do you mean by that?" said the Caterpillar sternly.
"Explain yourself!"
~ Lewis Carroll, Alice's Adventures in Wonderland

Cultural Emergency

I continue to work on environmental projects as well as social media and am fairly well known for both things, though I have not been successful at tying them together. As a marketing consultant who advises others on their branding and messaging, I find it increasingly difficult to explain my own.

Unsure of "what's next," I do another vision board. This time the clues lead me to the emerging field of study called social permaculture—in short, "the art of designing beneficial relationships." Permaculture is a portmanteau for permanent + agriculture, or now, the simpler "culture." I take an online permaculture design course and am disappointed when it does not delve deeply in social aspects.

I read everything I can find and study free online videos on my own. As I pursue this field of study very few have heard of and no one is begging me to do, my consulting work slows. In fact, 2017 is the least financially successful year of my working life. Yet, I persist.

Most of what I find about social permaculture seems to be written by Starhawk. I also find another author, Looby Macnamara, who has written *People and Permaculture*. In mid-November 2017 I learn that both Starhawk and Looby, along with Jon Young, another author I admire, will be teaching a workshop called Cultural Emergence in Oakland, California in January. My bank account has never looked so pitiful and I'm feeling the strain of some mounting bills. It seems crazy to think this is the right time to spend money on travel and a workshop, yet imaginal cells are telling me this is where I need to be to aid in my transformation. I see myself returning from the workshop with great information to benefit my community. I share my desire with my husband. "You have good ideas, you can make it happen" he encourages.

Often, people find their creativity expanding and their ideas flowering in the sunlight of energetic support. ~ Starhawk, The Empowerment Manual: A Guide for Collaborative Groups

One permaculture principle I find particularly helpful is "Integrate rather than segregate"—by putting the right things in the right place, relationships develop between them and they support each other. Picture a group of people from a bird's-eye view, holding hands in a circle together. The space in the center could represent "the whole being greater than the sum of the parts." The proverb "many hands make light work" suggests that when we work together, the job becomes easier.

I begin to think about who might be interested in learning about the material I will bring back from the workshop. A friend in California offers me lodging. A local Unity Church books me as their Sunday speaker for February 2018. I am scheduled for a book signing in May 2018 for a book that has not yet been written, much less published, about empowerment. Effectively, I pre-sell enough copies of my book to fund the trip! "It's like time travel!" exclaimed one supporter.

Time travel, indeed. I can't wait to write the next chapter of my journey through Wonderland!

ABOUT THE AUTHOR: Kathy Sipple resides just outside of Chicago near the Indiana Dunes with her husband John and their black Labrador retrievers, Bodhi and Pema. She is a frequent keynote speaker and trainer and host of 219 GreenConnect podcast. She holds a B.A. in Economics from the University of Michigan and is a member of Mensa. She won a Golden Innovator Award from Barbara Marx Hubbard and Conscious Evolutionaries Chicagoland for her empowering and groundbreaking work in social media. Sipple works online with clients everywhere to provide social media strategy, training, and coaching.

Kathy Sipple
Social Artist
kathysipple.com
kathy@cothrive.org
219-405-9482

Create Your Own Reality
Debbie Peever

"ONK, ONK, ONK." This is the familiar sound of my alarm going off at 4:44 am, a time I have intentionally set to remind myself of how far I have come in the past thirty years. This has become my current reality and I better darn well love it because it is exactly what I have created for myself.

At twenty-four, when I became a schoolteacher, it seemed a perfect fit for my lifestyle, which included a new husband with a ready-made family. Four years later, I gave birth to a beautiful baby girl, and eight years after that, I found myself divorced and a single parent.

The following year, I was diagnosed with Irritable Bowel Syndrome (IBS), leading to Crohns. At that time, there was little understanding of this condition, though stress and diet were believed to be the main triggers. Apparently, my ideal career was also the root cause of my condition. The treatments, which were largely untested and wholly unacceptable to me, included drugs with numerous side effects, regular, invasive testing, and possible surgeries. I was still reeling from my failed marriage and trying to raise my young daughter. What would I do now? How would I earn a living? And the biggest question: How could this be happening to me?

I began investigating alternative treatment options, which included everything from meditation and exercise for stress reduction to various nutritional regimens. Both posed their own challenges. There was very little information on gluten free, Non-GMO, organic, vegan and vegetarian diets, and meditation was only done in the lotus position. Sitting this way was not just uncomfortable for me, it was near impossible.

After a few months of trial and error I found things that worked:

no corn, no meat, limited wheat, reduced dairy, no cow's milk, reduced starches and sugars and less raw fruits and veggies. Eating smaller meals more often throughout the day, along with regular walking, light weight training and regular aerobic workouts at the gym were also helpful.

During this time I also began exploring my inner world and the circumstances that had led to my condition. I discovered that fear, ignorance, and misplaced loyalties had governed many of my life choices. I realized I'd chosen to become a teacher largely because my mother had been one. It had served her well; my mom was a single parent and teaching provided a good living, as well as ample time off to spend summers and school breaks with me.

My relationships with men had been heavily influenced by the dysfunctional relationship I had witnessed between my parents. I had listened to a lot of arguing, witnessed a fair number of physical altercations, and observed two people who spent time together out of obligation, necessity, and convenience. As an adult, I kept picking the same type of partner and repeating the scenarios I had lived as a young child.

My eating habits were dictated by old patterns as well. In my house, meals consisted of three squares per day and were made up of meat, potatoes, and veggies. Meal times were adhered to whether I was hungry or not and I was expected to eat everything on my plate or go without dessert. Yet despite this restrictive routine—or perhaps because of it—I learned to use "comfort" foods to mask or ease emotional and physical pain. Exercise was limited to ice skating in the winter and playing ball in the summer. There was no real physical education program at school or extracurricular activities. I was, for the most part, sedentary.

Somehow, I found myself reflecting on these circumstances from a place of opportunity and promise, rather than one of lack. These reflections ignited an awareness that pushed me to reshape, restructure, and recreate my reality based on my truth, rather than learned behavior and patterning. My self-perception began to shift from sick, unemployed, alone, undesirable, fat, and lazy to healthy, adventurous, and independent. I was beginning to understand that I could define the moments of my life instead of allowing moments to define me. Many of my relationships began to fall away and new, healthier ones were formed. It was during this time of self - discovery that I met my current husband.

The year 2007 was filled with defining moments. I'd read enough about Quantum Physics to know that everything in the universe is made up of energy that vibrates at a specific frequency. It was during a trip to Honduras, that I saw firsthand how powerful this theory really is.

The first leg of our trip was through Toronto. A case of air sickness caused us to delay our trip so that my husband could be medically checked out and given the okay to continue flying. Instead of travelling to Cancun, we were re-ticketed on a red-eye through Mexico City. At the boarding area, I encountered a man that appeared to be very fascinated with me. He made numerous attempts to interact, even seeking me out when I moved seats. I was so spooked by the experience that I took photos of this man and told my husband about them in case anything happened to me. Once on the plane, I saw the strange man was sitting in the row behind us! I somehow relaxed enough to fall asleep and by the time we landed I had forgotten about the whole ordeal. It was very early in the morning when we entered the terminal. The place was silent and aside from the people getting off the plane there was virtually no one in sight. Then, out of the blue, I heard a voice. I turned and found the strange man standing before me.

"Immigration is this way," he said.

"I'm going to the bathroom first," I blurted out without thinking.

It was only after my husband asked me why I would announce this to the very person who had creeped me out that some panic set in again. To my great relief, we got through immigration and a lengthy layover without running into my "stalker" again.

Things only got stranger once we arrived in Honduras. I could sense things that I had no business sensing and, as crazy as this sounds, I would get guidance to go a certain direction, or dig in the sand to find a beautiful shell for no apparent logical reason. One afternoon our guide took us to a local market. I was intrigued by the beauty of the items that were handcrafted by the women of this area. Our guide had a schedule to stick to, and became insistent on leaving; I was pulled to stop and admire the wares on my way out. As we were getting into the vehicle, we heard a loud crash. A three-car accident had occurred right outside the market, and had I ignored my urge to linger and left when our guide wanted us to, we would have been smack dab in the middle of it!

That trip heralded a profound, mysterious shift. I found a new love for crystals, candles, colors, and meditation. I made more time for me and continued to cultivate people and activities I could really connect with. Somewhere along the way my anxiety, discomfort, and fear inspired by the man on my flight had turned into acceptance, trust, and faith. I have often asked myself whether those few words exchanged in the airport terminal somehow set in motion those changes. Were the vibration and frequency of those words the catalyst? Had this communication and interaction shaped the appearance and uniqueness of what was now becoming my reality in the same way that research by Einstein and Telsa, Biofield technology and studies done around the world had confirmed how frequency and vibration organizes matter?

A few weeks later, my circumstances shifted again when Sue came into my world. Originally a major influence in my daughter's life, she became my friend, confidant, peer, and mentor. She introduced me to the "feather, feather, rock, logging truck" phenomena. Quantum Physics at its finest.

Feathers, she explained, are gentle nudges, tickling your awareness and softly pushing you in a direction. If negated or ignored the gentle nudges of *FEATHER, FEATHER* are then delivered in the punch, like a *ROCK* hitting your windshield. This is your wake-up call. It is so shocking that you become literally paralyzed for a moment, incapable of reacting. If previous attempts of *FEATHER, FEATHER* and *ROCK* have failed, a *LOGGING TRUCK* will completely change your world as you know it. This is the message that rips the proverbial rug out from under you and sends you spiraling. It is, as you can imagine, a very, very rough landing.

My failed marriage and IBS diagnosis fit this pattern very well, and I now realize that I had received guidance, red flags, and opportunities that, had I listened, might have diverted me from the devastating result. It is for this reason that I now pay closer attention to messages I am given.

Prior to my decision to begin a book in 2012, I had received many such prompts to become a writer. Each time the poke would carry a bit more punch, as the numerous boxes of my journals, articles, and research in my basement can attest. I believe that first attempt at writing was necessary to aid in the healing process that needed to occur between myself and my daughter. She was the only intended audience; I know this because to the best of my knowledge, I have never received any further messages to complete or publish that piece of work.

Did I continue to receive *Feather, Feather* to do more writing? Absolutely! The boxes in my basement multiplied and my mentor's words continually rang in my head every time I drew an oracle card indicating I had a book inside of me, every time a random (which by the way is *never* random) email would appear in my inbox about how to become a writer, and every time I was told by someone how helpful my words had been.

I continued to pay attention to the feathers, and in February 2016, I posted the first blog on my website. In May 2016, a Soul Realignment Reading revealed that my Divine Nature was to express myself through a variety of forms, including writing; and in November 2016, one of the participants at a Reiki Share, while working at my feet, blurted out, "Why am I seeing feathers...? Wait a minute there is a logging truck as well!" When I asked if there had been a rock, her reply was a very definite "NO." In January 2017, I began writing my second book, this time with the intention to publish, and in April 2017, a dear friend extended an invitation for me to be a part of this anthology. This was the gentle nudge I needed to finally step out of the "working on publishing something" mentality to actually doing it.

Since experiencing the ***LOGGING TRUCK*** in my twenties, I have made the decision to be more open to the guidance I receive. By eliminating procrastination, asking for more divine guidance, and believing in myself and those gentle nudges of the *Feather,* I now make necessary changes more willingly, rather than having the changes forced upon me. When my alarm goes off at 4:44, marking a new day and a new beginning, I am reminded that by connecting with the guidance given and paying attention to my intuition and inner wisdom, I am in harmony with the universe. Relinquishing the need for tight-fisted control, I have empowered myself to relax into the flow and receive the blessings the universe has in store for me; creating a reality filled with love, light, and happiness.

ABOUT THE AUTHOR: Debbie Peever is an intuitive healer, instructor, and owner of Northern Lights Holistic Health and Healing, which is nestled in the foothills of the Canadian Rockies in northern British Columbia. A Registered Reiki Master/Teacher, she is also certified in Aroma Touch Technique and Meridian Massage, trained in Craniosacral and Trigger Point Release and offers a variety of techniques to support the health and well-being of body, mind, and spirit. Debbie, who also holds a degree in Education, combines her experience as a classroom teacher with more than fifteen years of study in Holistic Healing practices to provide her clients with transformational workshops and programs.

Debbie Peever CACR™, BGS Ed, RT-CRA
Certified Angel Card Reader, Reg. Teacher Canadian Reiki Assn.
northernlightsholistichealthandhealing.ca
northernlightsholistichealth@gmail.com
facebook.com/northernlightsholistichealthandhealing

Empower Your Life:
Sojourner of Truth
Anita D. Russell

"To SOAR is to fly fearlessly with vision and purpose."

Isabella Baumfree was a woman on a quest, speaking the truth of who she was as an ex-slave, an anti-slavery orator, and an advocate for human rights. Her famous speech, "Ain't I a Woman?", was a powerful rebuke to those who sought to silence her arguments for women's rights. The moment she squeezed her way out of her mother's womb, she began a sojourn towards the truth of who she was destined to be—certainly not a slave. Perhaps she changed her name from Isabella Baumfree to Sojourner Truth to emphasize her quest for true identity.

Likewise, each of us is a sojourner of the truth of who we *really* are. As you grow and develop, you create a great life story while simultaneously searching for the voice to tell it. Sometimes you have to fight to find and be your true self—to experience your own true story and the ability to tell it in your own voice.

The key to finding your voice is to SOAR higher than your circumstances, fear, or limiting beliefs. SOAR is an acronym for *Step Out And Redesign* and the focus is on YOU, your accountability, your responsibility for the choices you make, and the consequences you reap, even when the circumstantial tide is against you. Mind you, I fully acknowledge that the circumstances of your life were initiated at birth. Your journey down the birth canal was certainly not of your own doing, the circumstances in which you were born indeed were beyond your control. I, personally, began as a wounded child.

I started life on Linden Avenue in East Pittsburgh, PA. I'm told that as an infant I spent about two weeks with my paternal grandmother. Then, for reasons never fully explained, my mother became estranged from that side of the family. Somewhere along the line I became conscious of the branch on the family tree that led to my father and my grandmother; then came the day at the post office when I saw my father's name and picture on an FBI wanted poster. In spite of this revelation, I still prayed that one day I would meet my grandmother *and* my father.

I spent most of my childhood with my mom and two younger brothers, though I started off with three younger siblings. In 1962, my family was shattered by the death of my three-year-old sister, Laney. In those days there was no supportive care for bereaved siblings and I suffered tremendously, mostly in silence, at the loss. At Laney's funeral, I had a vision and heard a voice whisper into my naïve spirit, like a friend, *I will never leave you.* Just five years old, I lacked the faculties to understand the vision or deal with the manifestation of all that grief, depression, and guilt, so I dragged it through my life for decades like a child holding onto the arm of a stuffed animal, all tattered and torn.

After the loss of my sister, a devastating house fire, and a subsequent move to Homestead, I sunk even further into silence. Behind closed doors, our new life included domestic violence along with physical and emotional damage. I suffered from functional depression, a form of inner life implosion that manifested mostly as superficial cutting on my wrists, and I grew from a wounded child to a suicidal teen. My life had become a wilderness journey; I had no idea what the other side would look like, or if I would even get there.

As an adult, things changed when I began a *real* walk with God and finally understood that vision at Laney's funeral. I had always loved the notion of God speaking to Moses face to face, as a man speaks to a friend, and that's how He had spoken to me all those years ago. Throughout my life, God has been a trusted friend, guiding me in the direction of purpose in spite of the multitude of detours I took. Thus I began to see my journey, not as one of pain and suffering, but of liberation and empowerment.

Getting to college was the first major milestone in my life, a true triumph in the end, though it did not feel like it in the beginning. I always knew I would continue my education beyond high school, I just wasn't sure of the path. I take that back, I *thought* I was sure, dreaming of a career as a pediatrician and saving lots of children. The error of my dream was an unseen motivation driven by the guilt of not being able to save my sister. (Obviously, pursuing a medical career with guilt as a primary motivation is just not a good idea.)

I was about to enter Penn State University as a pre-med major when I heard God's voice again. *This is not what you're supposed to be doing.* I was much older then and those words sounded like a warning to me. In an instant I decided I better not take a detour this time. After a gap year of working, I began my freshman year at the University of Pittsburgh.

During my years at Pitt I reached several personal milestones. Freshman year, I *finally* got to stand in the same room with my grandmother, known in her family as Nanny. I was immediately enthralled with her and ecstatic when I was invited to join my newfound family over Christmas break. Our initial meeting was at a bus station in Philadelphia where my grandmother so lovingly said, "You look just like your father." Even now, I get goosebumps when I think of that moment.

I spent the following summer living with Nanny and getting to know the family. Nanny told me all about my father. Turns out I have siblings in California and Pittsburgh, and though I have yet to stand in the same room with my father, we are vicariously connected through those siblings.

In the meantime, I found myself still drawn to the medical field and later participated in a summer work program targeting science, nursing, and pre-med majors. As a rising junior, I spent the summer working at the Allegheny County Coroner's Office assisting with autopsies. This was also the summer that Grandaddy passed away and I prayed that an autopsy would not be needed. And I saw a different side of my mother as she suffered the grief of losing her father.

During the summer of 1979, while working as a research intern at the University of Pittsburgh Medical School, I finally found my niche. After graduating in 1980, I pursued a research career in academia, eventually moving into the pharmaceutical industry as a drug discovery scientist at Bristol-Myers Squibb in New Jersey.

One thing I have learned on my sojourn of truth is that when God gives you lemons, He *intends* for you to make lemonade. After spending ten years as a drug discovery scientist, the lemonade turned out to be an assignment in learning and development, taking me out of the lab and into a larger role managing the Center for Science Education at BMS. This transition in 2000 launched my career as a learning and development professional. Thirteen years later, the lemonade was early retirement and soaring as an entrepreneur. Like my life itself, my career has been a fluid one, flowing from research to learning and development to entrepreneurship.

Reflections on years of circumstances, choices, and consequences served as the inspiration for the SOAR concept, which I developed in 2014. In stepping out and redesigning my own life, the following ten values sprung from the realization that along the way I had become liberated from fear, doubt, and limiting beliefs.

10 SOAR Values:

1. Faith, trust, belief – everyone has faith, trust, and belief in something or someone. A well-integrated life includes a spiritual domain reflecting a partnership with God through faith, trust, and belief. Fun, freedom, and fulfillment is the destination of a well-integrated life. Fun comes by experiencing the joys of life through faith. Freedom comes by the trust you place in your vision and purpose. Fulfillment comes when you have a belief system that includes service and connection to others.

2. Vision, purpose, action – vision empowers purpose and the fulfillment of purpose is impossible without action. Vision is the "where" of your life; that is, not where you are but where you are going. It's not just what you see but *how* you see things, like joy, pain, people, God. Vision also empowers purpose, the "why" of your personal journey with a focus on something greater than yourself. However, one must recognize that fulfillment of purpose is impossible without executing a plan of action.

3. Life transitions – the dynamics of circumstances, choices, and consequences bring about change. Making the choice to redesign your life interconnects with changing circumstances and emergent consequences. Essentially, redesigning your life is related to life transitions, either major or minor in scope.

How you manage those transitions cumulatively and progressively over time determines the outcome.

4. Managing relationships – a core element of growth and development. Building, maintaining, and sustaining relationships is a skill set that involves ongoing effort and commitment to establish a solid foundation over time. Managing relationships is a key to success in your spiritual, personal, and business life.

5. Community and family – contribute and make a difference. This value reflects the desire to have an impact and to make a difference in the lives of others. Serving families and communities is about stewardship—building quality relationships, being in service to others based on their needs, and using your influence to bring about positive change by building diverse relationships, engaging in community service, and creating memorable experiences.

6. Personal economy – unique, constantly changing based on what matters to you. While everyone pays attention to the national and global economies, never forget that it's personal too. Your personal economy is unique, constantly changing, mirroring things that truly matter to you—your family, your home, your passions, your career. Life transitions and milestone events force us to re-evaluate our personal economy as life progresses.

7. Continuous improvement – make it a lifelong endeavor. This SOAR value is about personal development motivated by a mindset of improvement through learning. Personal development is a process of self-improvement through continuous learning, skill enhancement, setting and achieving goals and objectives. Continuous improvement activities are self-determined, self-directed, and self-monitored.

8. Creativity – it's never depleted; the more you use the more you have. This value embodies an extra edge, the desire to share your life experiences and lessons learned through the creative process. For many the process of redesigning life has led to the discovery of artistry and creativity that benefits and impacts others or inspires change. Creativity is reflected in the work of visual artists, performance artists, writers, poets, craftsmen, designers, musicians, scientists, and others who engage in the creative process in their life endeavors.

9. Fluid living – nurture your mind, body, and spirit holistically. A fluid lifestyle means taking care of your mind, body, and spirit to achieve a holistic approach to wellness living. Your lifestyle influences the overall shape of your life, that is an integration of your spirit, heart, abilities, personality, and experiences. The lessons you learn and the choices you make influence the shape of your life.

10. Legacy – the legacy we leave behind is a true reflection of the life we have led. The things you do for others, the lives you touch, your influence on those around you, and the impact you make is your legacy. Creating an inter-generational legacy is a life-long endeavor designed by the plans and the choices you make along the way. Your influence *is* your legacy; make it good.

Today, I live a fluid lifestyle, based on these valuable lessons learned. In the process I have discovered not only the voice to tell my story with transparency and honesty, but my life purpose: to help other sojourners of their own truth.

ABOUT THE AUTHOR: Anita D. Russell was born and raised in Pittsburgh, PA. Her fluid life spans multiple disciplines, including ministry, pharmaceutical R&D, learning and development, web design, e-learning design, and youth and community leadership. Now working independently, Anita is the founder and creator of The Place to SOAR and SOAR Travel Ministry. She is also a John Maxwell Team life coach and a writer. Anita was first published as a contributing author in *Motherhood Dreams and Success: You can Have It All*, an anthology filled with inspiration and wisdom by a diverse group of women from around the world.

Anita D. Russell
The Place to SOAR
theplacetosoar.com
anitarussell@theplacetosoar.com
609-837-7237

Hair Today, Gone Tomorrow
My Story of Release and Healing
Jane Del Piero

It began on our trip to Playa Hermosa, Costa Rica. After a beautiful evening of dinner and music with some friends, I lay in the arms of my beloved husband and let the rhythmic sound of the waves carry me off to sleep. That's when my perfect vacation quickly spiraled out of control. Wild, terrifying nightmares, coupled with waves of nausea and a feeling of dis-ease, invaded my sleep, then I woke to find myself soaking wet, lying in a pool of sweat. *Why do I hear music playing in the house?* I got up to investigate, and with each step I could feel the nausea building as my body alternated between intense sweats and chills.

I was still trying to find the source of the music when a violent wave of nausea and intense heat consumed me. After a round of projectile vomiting, I began praying to GOD and my guardian angels for help, support, and protection. Intense emotions, memories, losses, traumas, and painful experiences flooded my mind, and I felt an intense desire to release the karma, the stories and all the trapped energies from deep within my core. *What is this? The healer experiencing a healing crisis?*

I began systematically analyzing the inventory of my spiritual bank account, clearing off one by one all disappointments, hurts, the painful and traumatic events of my life. *Finding my father dead in a pool of blood.* Boom! A massive tidal wave of emotions crashed over me, setting off another round of uncontrollable vomiting, and a loss of control of all bodily functions. Slowly, I crawled toward the couch and for the next few minutes felt some semblance of peace. Then, in the distance, I heard the music again. This time it's the memory of my *stepfather* dying. I got the news while at school, just before a basketball game. Before I knew it, I was moving toward the bathroom again, gripped with an overwhelming nausea.

Jane, I deeply love and accept you, you have the strength to overcome all challenges… I chanted this to myself over and over, like a mantra, as I stumbled back to the couch and collapsed, exhausted. I'd barely drifted off to sleep when it started again. *Disgusted, violent, attacked, and unable to move…I witnessed myself being violated.* Electrically shocked to a standing position, I projectile vomited three times on my way to the bathroom. *"GOD, PLEASE HELP ME."* Completely overcome by emotions, I cried uncontrollably as I cleaned myself up and headed for the kitchen. I took an ice cube and placed it in my mouth, but even this small amount of fluid set off more waves of nausea. I grabbed my Bach Flower Essence Rescue Remedy, placing a few drops under my tongue and rubbing it on my heart and pulse points.

I felt myself relaxing, deeper and deeper, as I released traumatic memories trapped within my core… until I fell asleep. Instantly I was in a dream space, with people yelling—*someone yelling at me*, sending waves of terror and panic through my body; I witnessed atrocities, experienced the suffering of humanity. Jolts of electricity rushed through my body as memories of being violated, persecuted, judged, killed, and harmed in other lifetimes burst forth and with them, highly toxic emotions. Suddenly, I heard my guardian angel, Archangel Michael, say to me, "You are being given the opportunity to completely recreate and reformat who you are."

This process would continue for the next fourteen hours, completely cleansing my heart and soul in what seemed to be a reformatting of my cellular memory, before I finally fell into a deep sleep. Six hours later I awoke feeling very weak, and recounted the events of the night before to my horrified husband before heading to the shower. There, I got another shock—my hair falling out in clumps! Telling myself it was the stress of the night before, I returned to bed, utterly exhausted. I started chanting to myself over and over and over: *I allow myself to heal, healing is good for me and others. I release all that no longer serves my highest and best good. I release. I release. I release.* It was the only way I felt safe.

The following day at the health food store, I noticed a number of individuals looking very weak and wiped out. I ran into a construction worker who was putting the new pool in at my home

—he told me that his daughter was deathly ill and his wife had also been sick for two days. Another woman heard us talking and told us that she and three friends had been out to eat dinner on the beach and woke up that night violently ill. They were still struggling physically and emotionally. Then, unbelievably, an elderly couple approached and told us they had been hearing similar stories over and over for the last two days.

I was still trying to absorb this shocking string of "coincidences" when my gaze landed on a water purification system for sale. Instantly I was struck by the memory of the water truck down in a dirty hole, pulling up water that they later sold to the restaurants! Horrified, I realize that the water had been used to rinse the vegetables that had made me and numerous other people very sick.

Three days later, my husband and I returned to the United States. As the days turned into weeks, I noticed more and more of my hair falling out, breaking off, and looking dry and damaged; there were even small bald spots all over my scalp. My stress levels began to climb. Every morning I would awake to find hair covering my pillow, which only led to more stress, and, inevitably, more hair loss. Desperate for answers, I began seeing doctors and shamans alike, and of course chanting my mantras each day.

I received numerous wacky diagnoses, including alopecia, female balding pattern, and hypothyroidism, before figuring out that my thyroid was yo-yoing from hyper to hypo back to hyper, wreaking havoc on my metabolism and kidneys. Apparently, the thyroid was thrown into turmoil when my body tried to expel the toxic water, and now my system was swimming with parasites and bacteria. *WHAT???* In addition to a strict regimen of antibiotics, I focused on my meditation and yoga and treated myself as gently as possible. Slowly, the thyroid began to regulate.

At this time I also had an epiphany while in meditation. I witnessed myself engaging with my clients over the years and saw that I needed to create clearer boundaries in order to keep myself clear of their traumas. I also realized that it was time to tell the victim to get lost and create a different story. I was, after all, a warrior! That day, I set out on a journey of self-love and healing, and the first step—and one of the most painful—was to decide whether to keep the long hair that remained or cut it all off.

When I moved into my heart, I got my answer: it was time to stop stressing, release the story, and let go of the old karma. I had wasted too many hours, days, weeks, and months filled with anxiety, stressing over what people thought about me and judging myself as worthless. This had to stop completely, once and for all. I had to invest in and care about myself as much as I cared for others. Several agonizing snips later, the twenty-four inches of red curly hair was gone and so was the person I used to be. It was devastating—I didn't even recognize myself when I looked in the mirror. Even as I sobbed, I heard my higher self say, "Jane, I deeply love and accept you, and you have the strength to overcome all challenges." I knew in that moment that I needed to fall madly, deeply in love with myself, and find forgiveness and compassion for those I had trespassed against and those that had trespassed against me. This dark night of the soul would be my catalyst for healing.

I wrote myself a prescription for deep recovery. For me, this meant spending a month at Shiva Tattva, an ashram in Rishikesh, India, about six hours north of Delhi. I needed to accept what had happened and adjust to the new me without having to see everyone in my small community.

At the ashram, each day began at 5:30 a.m. for mediation, followed by an hour and half of Hatha yoga. After a breakfast of oats and fruit, I would take an hour-long walk, then head off to morning mantra class. We broke midday for a pure, clean, delicious lunch, then went to a philosophy of yoga class, followed by another hour and a half of yoga. Dinner was one Indian delight or another. I allowed myself to melt into the routine and quiet my mind with no television, no work, no cellphone, and no crazy questions from other people—"Jane you had the most beautiful hair, why would you ever cut it off?"—to distract me.

I pretty much kept to myself, just allowing the healing energy to saturate my cells. Each evening, I'd walk down the hill, take a small boat across the Ganges River, and make my way to Aarti on the Ganges. A powerful and uplifting spiritual ritual that uses fire as an offering, Ganga Aarti is performed at dusk at the three holy cities of Haridwar, Rishikesh, and Varanasi. During the ritual I would release my sorrow, my pain, my suffering, and traumas to Mother Ganga. It was critical to my healing, and helped me leave

India empowered, healthy, and on my road to recovery.

This has been one of the hardest journeys I've ever embarked upon. We don't realize how much of our identity is tied up in our hair until we lose it. Your hair is one of the first things people see when they look at you and one of the first things you notice when you look at yourself in the mirror. Eventually, I stopped obsessively touching my hair, and was able to go out in public with my head uncovered and feel safe. I learned that I am not my hair, but a beautiful woman who carries the energy of a warrior. I also learned to deeply love and respect myself, and to love and honor myself for the dedication to my health.

Now, one year later, my hair is growing back, thick, curly, a beautiful dark red hue, and very healthy. I held tightly to my faith, believed fully in myself, and with the support of my family, friends, and spirit guides I was able to persevere. I never once lost hope and belief that I could recover from such a physically draining event. I choose to invest in myself daily, to love, honor and respect myself, and move forward everyday toward health, happiness, joy, and bliss. I bow humbly in infinite gratitude for this amazing life and all the lessons I have learned. Namaste.

ABOUT THE AUTHOR: Jane Del Piero is a Medicine Woman, Modern Day Shaman, Acupuncturist, Nutritionist, Sound healer, Ascension, and Soul Path Transformational Guide. She helps individuals heal everyday aches and pains, then dives deeper to facilitate a personal journey that allows them to step into their own power and truth by releasing self-doubts, limiting beliefs, and fears, and old patterns and behaviors that no longer serve them. Jane is also a co-host of The Wild Women's Circle in Telluride, Colorado; the creator of Sacred Hoop, a monthly shamanic and ceremonial class; and a Kundalini / Tantra yoga instructor.

Jane Del Piero
LuvLight LLC
luvlight.net
jane@luvlight.net
303-807-8355

The Power in Choosing YOU!
Fiona Johnson

"Courage is not the absence of fear, but rather the judgement that something else is more important than fear." ~ J. N. Hollingworth

Life does not offer many guarantees, and you never know what lies on the other side of each door you attempt to open. What's important is that you find the courage to *walk through* those doors, for if you don't, the things you desire most will continue to elude you.

It was a Saturday evening in mid-November 2003, and I was on my way to a meeting. As I drove my thoughts drifted to a few weeks earlier, when the man I'd thought I was going to spend the rest of my life with told me he had found someone else. "It's serious," he'd said, and they were moving in together. Words could not explain my shock, brokenness, hurt, and disappointment—in one fell swoop he had taken away not only my present, but my future as well. Since that day I had been wallowing in despair, self-pity, and isolation, and it was getting me nowhere. I needed a way to escape, far from my nightmare where I could begin to live again. That's when I started contemplating a move to the States. This was a terribly difficult decision. Though my life in Jamaica was far from perfect, it was all I had known for the first twenty-nine years of my life. I had no idea what lay behind "Door Number 2."

I had begun reflecting on my life, what it was, and what I would like it to be. In my daydreams I created a world of light and laughter, a life of many firsts. My first job, my first real love, my first kiss, my first walk on the beach, or my first home; somewhere to belong and someone to belong to, who would love me unconditionally and accept me for me. The thoughts of all these firsts made the desire inside of me that much stronger. The excitement began to mount and my vision started to take on a life of its own.

It wasn't until that evening in November, though, that it suddenly struck me: I had to do it. It was as though something had gone off inside me—an internal alarm so loud I can still remember the exact mile marker on the road when I "heard" it.

The streets of Kingston were buzzing with weekend festivities, with people from all walks of life moving merrily about streets aglow with multicolored lights. The very smell of Christmas was in the air. It was a scene as familiar as my own reflection, but I had never before felt such absolute clarity. And that clarity was telling me that in order to have the future I wanted, I would have to leave everything I knew behind. I needed to find a place that would allow me to leave the past behind and make room for those new possibilities. For the first time in forever I was finally choosing me, I was convinced this was it; this was my time.

Fueled by this newfound courage, the next day I picked up the phone and called my aunt in Florida. I informed her of my plans and asked if I could live with her until I got settled. Thankfully, she agreed (sigh) and the next thing I knew my move was scheduled for right after Christmas. There was no turning back.

Just when I thought I had it all figured out, without warning, fear began to raise its ugly head: *Are you crazy? Giving up your job, your apartment, your car, your friends, and your support system?* My mind was filled with what-ifs, and it took every ounce of courage not to abort my plans. I prayed harder than ever for reassurance but the uncertainty was now giving me sleepless nights. Realizing that I needed to confront these fears head-on, I did the one thing I knew would seal this move. At first light I put out a notice that I was having a garage sale—everything must go!

I remember lying on my couch watching television when someone knocked on my door and literally bought that couch out from under me. Someone else wanted my television, then my stove, then my microwave, and suddenly, my living room and dining area was as empty as the day I moved in. There was truly no turning back! I begged the person buying my bedroom furniture to let me keep it for one more week until I left, but she said—you guessed it, NO—and that's when I found myself sleeping at a friend's apartment. As scary as it was, I was forcing myself to let go of my fears, move on to something new and not look back.

Not a day went by that I didn't question my decision. In the confines of my borrowed space I cried myself to sleep and longed for the comfort of the love I once had, for someone to reassure me that this new chapter in my life would be worth it. Instead I hugged my pillow, found peace in prayer, hope in my spiritual walk, and joy in knowing that He who is able would never leave me to walk this journey alone.

Finally, the big day arrived. I bid farewell to my family and friends, boarded my flight, and went off in search of all my firsts. I landed at Fort Lauderdale International Airport and although I had made this journey many times before—this was very different. Florida was no longer a vacation destination; it was now my home. There were so many emotions rushing through my head and heart, but if I had to sum them up in one word it would be *bittersweet*. On the one hand I was thrilled and excited to start my new life; on the other, I had no car, no job, and limited funds to get me by. I was a stranger in someone else's world and figuring out how to navigate it would be no easy feat.

Though I was welcomed with open arms, I could not deny the reality that I had given up my own home to share a room with my aunt. There were days that I longed for my own space, where I could close the doors and pretend everything was great. Less than a month after my move my thirtieth birthday came around, and my emotions were at an all-time high. Most women at this stage would be settled in a career and married, their futures mapped out, while I had nothing. After a call from my mother—during which I dutifully lied about how well I was doing—the phone rang again; this time it was three of my closest friend/sisters I'd met in high school. They never forgot a birthday, and that day it seemed they were especially happy and bubbly and loud on the other end of the line. More homesick than ever, all I could do was cry in silence on my end. When they realized I was not laughing along they quieted down and asked what was wrong. I tried to muster the courage to tell them I was doing great, but I could not lie to them as easily as

I could my mom. Instead, I hurried them off the phone, got into bed, and cried myself to sleep. Thankfully, my aunt worked that night so at least I had the room all to myself.

The next couple of months were productive: I opened my first bank account, got my driver's license and mobile phone; it didn't even take long to find my first job, paying the exact salary I'd prayed for. This was a blessing, for it opened doors that allowed me to experience many of the "firsts" I had dreamed off. Yes, I experienced the highs and lows, the what-ifs and the what-have-I-done days, but there were many happy days as well—days of meeting new people, making friends, learning a new culture and finally, experiencing a sense of belonging.

After two years in my new homeland I was heading to college; a few years after that I moved into my new apartment, and yes, I was basking in the love I had found in my first real relationship. I had prayed for this kind of love my entire adult life, and to see it show up when I least expected it was one of the greatest blessings God has ever bestowed upon me. My husband has lit a fire inside of me, one that seems to burn brighter with each passing day. He is the most accessible person I have ever met; he allows me to be myself and sees the beauty in me even on my worst days. He has created a safe space for me not only in his arms but in our home. Even in all my daydreams I never imagined loving or being loved in this way. I have often wondered what I ever did to deserve it, but as it turned out he too was praying for the love I had to offer. God saw fit to bless us with each other, and for that we are forever grateful.

Moving to the U.S. took an enormous leap of faith, but it has been the single most rewarding thing I have ever done. I have travelled to places and countries I'd only read about, immersed myself in various cultures and ate food I never knew existed; I have seen more things and experienced all my desired "firsts" and then some. There is so much joy in life, but we must show up and be present in the moments to see them. Too often we allow ourselves to miss the little things in search of the big things, when the truth is the little things are as equally important and hold memories to last a life time. Embracing change is not easy; it requires us to take a chance on life, and on ourselves. I've learned that it is often our darkest moments—when we are experiencing pain and disappointment—that are also the greatest opportunities for acceptance, growth, healing, transformation, and empowerment. That's what happened to me as I drove in Kingston that night all those years ago—I found the courage not only to open doors but the audacity to walk through them, and in the process I found myself. There is power in choosing you, and in believing that your dreams matter.

There are many different paths to success, but you must commit to finding the one that best suits you, then take that first step. It can be terrifying and painful, but I can guarantee that once you decide to show up others will show up and walk with you or lend you a helping hand along the way. There will be many twists and turns, but nothing worth having comes without challenges—your battle scars are just a part of your story. They make you special, set you apart, and shape you into who you were born to be. Remember, it's already in your DNA, all you have to do is activate it.

ABOUT THE AUTHOR: Fiona Johnson is a Consultant, certified Life Coach, Motivational Speaker, and Mentor with a passion for guiding others to discover their core value and to stand in their truth. She earned her Coaching Certification from Work Life Destination and her DISC Facilitator Certification from DISCcert Inc.; she also holds a Pre-Law Degree from Broward College; and B.A. in Psychology from Florida Atlantic University. Fiona is the founder of Speak Hope International, an organization dedicated to bringing hope to the hopeless and guiding their clients to realign their perspective to recognize the greatness in themselves. Fiona lives in Tamarac, Florida.

Fiona Johnson
Speak Hope International
speakhopeintl.com
pursuit@speakhopeintl.com
954-991-9155

Asking and Knowing Myself

Sharon Plaché

Many stories start with "Once upon a time..." Mine begins with "As long as I can remember..." and tells of my lifelong fascination with what I call the "big why." It encompasses all the questions about myself, my life, and the world around me that I would like to explore and understand. Asking and answering the "big why" has revealed much of who I am, why I am, where I am, when I am, what I am, how I am, and for what purpose. This self-inquiry and reflection are in my DNA, for sure, and have been very empowering and enlightening processes for me. Over the years, they have helped me become keenly aware of the talents, gifts, attributes, and virtues bequeathed to me by my ancestors. For this, I am eternally grateful. My part has been to recognize these gifts, honor them, utilize them and continue to grow with them as they support me.

I returned to the "big why" while pondering empowerment and what it means in my life. Why become empowered or fully resourced, truly Sourced? Can I recognize in each situation, encounter, and creation in my life that I am fully resourcing myself?

Even more than the "why," there is the "what." There have been certain vignettes in my life that gave me feedback from which to grow and learn. Whatever else these experiences were, they have been opportunities for continued personal inquiry, offering greater insight that led to self-empowerment.

The first of these was successfully navigating that initial, very challenging journey of the human experience: birth. I chose life, to breathe and create. Yes there was struggle, pressure, discomfort, and even a shock at the onset, but—hurrah!—I was here, fully alive, and ready to take each level as it presented itself. In that moment I said "Yes" to life, to the wonder and all else possible on this plane. I felt empowered.

Growing up with three brothers made a survivor out of me. Though their ridicule of the feminine was at times torturous, I am a stronger woman for it. Looking back, I realize my childhood was a rich and purposeful place to learn and grow in femininity and see the contrasts between the male and female manner and mind. I also learned to respect men–a good thing in what we often refer to "a man's world"! In fact, I discovered far more with these guys than I would have on my own. They all have distinct personalities and very unique lives, and with them, I have been able to step into completely different worlds and witness masculine self-expression. Yes, I chose them and the value of our shared experience has been empowering.

My upbringing in a very dogmatic and strict religious environment, with its patriarchal model of God, was also an important part of the "big why." Through this structured, legalistic belief system I learned a lot about how "not" to treat others and myself. But my real takeaway was learning about the inner workings of mind control, hierarchy, and power over people. From this I was able to step beyond this limited paradigm and create a truly authentic spiritual relationship with my Higher Power and Self. Through it I found a freedom to tune in and birth my own voice, my truth, and my connections to what is meaningful. This process required me to come to know myself and what I wanted to create in life. I have gratitude for the empowering journey that allowed me to clarify what was deep and authentic within myself.

I also had the opportunity to ponder the true face of God, and the Divine in me as a woman. I came to honor the reality of God as the whole of human expression, beyond gender and other limited forms or definitions. I came to love diversity and am grateful for all the paths that lead to Self-knowledge and its relationship with the Divine. Being able to honor my preference, free of dogma about what is the best, what is the only or even the ultimate, was truly empowering.

My time in the rigorous world of ballet was one of my greatest teachers. Learning to connect and master the body, mind, spirit, and emotions was a great test of self-discovery. The ballet world is a very exclusive, competitive, and superior-minded place. There can be an imbalanced pursuit of perfection, which takes a toll on one's health, family, relationships, self-worth, and perspective. Through this experience I realized there are many ways to test ourselves and excel. I also gained deeper understanding of the cost of success and learned I could choose to do what I wanted without sacrifice and suffering. This was empowering.

When I was young my family moved a lot, both in the United States and internationally. There is always an adjustment adapting to other cultures and lifestyles, and I was forced to learn, explore more, and get comfortable in my discomfort. I was empowered by the knowledge that I could resource myself in any situation and feel at home within myself regardless of the external environment.

That said, deciding to attend college and university after having isolated myself with dance was a huge decision. I was once again completely out of my comfort zone. It was all new—classes, student housing, friends, work-study programs, activities, clubs, and of course, the desire to excel academically. After one year at a small women's college, I realized I needed a bigger framework for my personal growth and transitioned to a four-year university. I began to see more clearly what life had to offer through education, creative thinking, laughter, love, and unlimited interests. I studied humanities, public relations, and business. I even became part of a regular program on the campus television station, president of the business club, and sang and toured with the concert choir.

After graduating, I spent the next four years exploring the corporate world of fashion. I was curious to see what it had to offer since I was drawn to the drama and creative arts. Just another version of "show time," as we say. I had begun to see what I didn't want in life and was now looking to see what other options there were for me. This experience would help clarify my need to honor myself and my abilities; I started looking at what compromises I was willing to make in order to please others rather than my intrinsic truth. I felt empowered with this discovery.

In 1989 I chose a rather uncommon path: the healing arts. It was a time when this was not considered a viable career, yet I felt the surge of the pioneer and entrepreneurial spirit of my ancestors. Through my studies, I came to a greater appreciation and purpose for self-healing and how this knowledge could benefit not only me but others as well. The choice gave me many wide-open vistas of possibility to explore. I have never looked back. If I had, I wouldn't have been able to keep looking forward.

Taking the risk to love and marry, only to have it end in divorce, is wrenching. Yet it too had a purpose. In choosing to uncouple and live the truth of who I was becoming was very empowering. The new version of me lived alone and really got to know who I was and why I choose what I choose. In other words, I couldn't hide from myself at all. Many of my female role models had given up a good portion of themselves to take care of and support their mate or someone else. I realized I was looking for a different dynamic, but figuring out what that looked like would take some time, and I took that time for myself now. Making a commitment to oneself is undoubtedly one of the best learning experiences, for we become both the student and the teacher. I learned that relationships with others—partners, lovers, or friends—would be successful only if I continued to allow myself the freedom of choice. This process of self-care continues today, in my current marriage, and the journey of loving myself while loving another has certainly added to my moments of inquiry as I search for the answer to the "big why."

I continue to be a student of life and remain curious about what else could be possible. This is a real key of empowerment for me. It seems I am always finding something else to explore or create, be it in personal growth or the arts, nature, or science. There is magic and life force energy in keeping a "beginner's mind," and I love seeing how everything fits into a bigger whole and is interrelated. Seeing myself in the context of OTHER is vastly helpful.

In 2008 I was faced with the need to undergo major back surgery. It was unexpected, to say the least. I knew when I was dancing there was an issue but never dreamed it would be this involved. The surgery was prefaced by severe pain in the back and leg from a physical abnormality that had led to an injury. I learned so much from being in a vulnerable position and relying on the kindness and support of others! I learned what it is like to be disabled and what it takes to heal. I have completely recovered and seem to be stronger in every way. Now *that* is empowering.

Recognizing the strength I had gained up to this point made me want to create a healing retreat space. I found out what it is like to actually manifest a vision or dream into reality. The space consists of a warm salt-water therapy pool outfitted with a deck for relaxation, bathhouse, sauna, cabana for massage, meditation garden and more. I call this "the pool that love built." It was a process for me of bringing something into existence from a heart space. I would encourage anyone to set an intention and see their dream come alive. It takes focus, knowing your boundaries, and being sure of what you want to create; however, there is nothing more empowering than to feel the power of creating in love, through love, and for love, for the highest good of all.

All of these experiences have given me a deeper understanding of what it is to be in a state of cause rather than effect. I don't look back. I no longer blame. I realize everything is my creation. It is valuable to know that being the creator self is where the flow happens and the empowerment is realized. The power of choice is infinite. There is love, laughter, discovery, and fun in being free to embrace all situations along the learning curves of life.

I now know all my preferences are purposeful. I see that more than ever. The freedom to express my desires gave me a deeper resolve to continue to create with no need to be opinionated or defensive. I became and continue to become the next best version of myself in honoring my needs, wants, and desires. They can be elevated as divine purpose, knowing they came from a true and authentic place.

As I continue to face my fears and move through them I find a greater sense of well-being. I am empowered as a woman, daughter, sibling, auntie, friend, dancer, student, partner, artist, business owner, mentor, teacher, and co-creator with the All That Is. May we all come to know how amazing and empowered we all are. Namaste.

ABOUT THE AUTHOR: Sharon Plaché is a creative and caring intuitive teacher, mentor, and healer. She has been in the Healing Arts since 1989. She is a practitioner, mentor, and teacher of ThetaHealing®, Innerwise®, NLP and MER®. Her retreat center in San Diego offers classes, trainings, aquatic bodywork, therapeutic massage, yoga, meditation and more. She is grateful to be a practitioner for the Wave Academy, which offers support to Veterans with PTSD. She is passionate about empowering clients to discover, grow, and create in all areas of life. Her combined thirty-five years of education and varied life experience gives her compassion and commitment.

Sharon Karise Plaché
SharonPlache.com
info@sharonplache.com
facebook.com/SharonPlache1
619-339-8177

Darkness Has Its Teaching

Jessica Tucker

When I first learned of the opportunity to contribute to this book, my reaction was fear. I had told those closest to me that I was sexually assaulted, but this was very different. This was going public, bearing my most painful experience for all to see. The thought was terrifying. But then I realized that even stronger than the fear was my need to share my story and hopefully help others understand that there is life after being violated, assaulted, or raped. Once I connected with the desire to be of service, taking part in this project became an honor and a privilege. Then the question became, how do I approach this? After careful contemplation I decided that rather than focusing on the event itself, it was more important to discuss the feelings and thoughts that came afterward, and how spiritual intervention saved my life.

That said, I do feel it is important to share some of the details. During the attack, I felt as if my soul had left my body, which is to say that along with the fear I felt a terrible emptiness. The expression "like a deer caught in headlights" took on a whole new meaning—the normal fight or flight response failed me, and I was frozen, unable to run away from approaching danger.

Suddenly, I heard a voice inside my head demanding that I tell him to stop before it got a hell of a lot worse and harder for me to come back from. I remained frozen, but the voice persisted. I finally told him to get the hell out of me, but it was too late. Those ten minutes of inaction were enough to send me down the rabbit hole.

After he left I went to bed feeling numb yet like a piece of me was missing—I just didn't know what that piece was. I slept, but kept jerking awake. I felt fearful. I felt empty. I felt *different*. When I woke I took a shower so hot the water burned my skin; it seemed the only way to get rid of the filth that seemed to cover every inch of me. I felt I needed to shed my skin to be me again. I thought nothing could be as bad as what had happened. I thought that right up until the moment I ran into him.

He smiled and leaned in to kiss me, not seeming to notice that I turned my cheek toward him so he wouldn't get near my lips. Now I felt crazy as well; I must be, or why else would he be acting as if everything was okay? It made me question what had actually happened. Was I making it up? Overreacting? *What's wrong with me?* These thoughts chased each other inside my mind as I tried to understand what was going on. Right after this encounter I managed to make my way to my classroom, where my students were waiting, grateful that they had a final exam and I could just sit there and not interact with anyone.

In the days that followed, I went about my normal schedule, but everything I did, whether it was walking to work or speaking with a colleague, was done on autopilot. Smiling was incredibly difficult, for what could there possibly be to smile about? Smiling was an act of feeling, and for me it was safest to feel nothing.

And still, it got worse. The first person I told was an older woman, who told me things like that happen and to just "get over it." I started smoking and drinking heavily. Eventually, I told other friends—some who stood by me and others who turned their backs. Some made comments insinuating that it was my fault. I had asked for it by inviting him into my room; I had *definitely* asked for it if I had been drinking (which I wasn't), or by hanging out with him if he was drinking (he'd had a few). I'd asked for it by not stopping him as soon as he started kissing me (in fact I had asked him to stop until he held me down), and of course I'd asked for it because I couldn't recognize the rapist within him. I'd asked for it by being too nice to people.

Initially, I sought help, but eventually these comments (including those from a psychologist!) weighed me down to the point that I thought I deserved to suffer the consequences. I also got plenty of commentary about my choices in the aftermath— "You should do this," and "Don't do that," et cetera—which left me feeling even more powerless, as if I didn't know how to handle being sexually assaulted properly. As if there is a proper way to handle being sexually assaulted! I would have to learn on my own that there is no right or wrong—it's an individual journey that must be respected and supported. But that realization came later.

I felt very much alone and unsafe in my place. I slept with a knife until a friend found out and came over for a sleepover. She helped me to stand up to the guy and I wrote him a message. I felt empowered afterward, but then the feelings started to boil to the surface—Feelings of shame, guilt, anger, and violent visions towards the guy who had ripped apart my world. They could not be hidden by numbness; they could not be held back by hot showers that left my skin red. They could not be ignored and this time they wanted to shout out loud and be noticed…Yet still, I hid from them. I smoked more and I drank more. I started to have sex with random guys—anything to keep the pain at bay.

That only works for so long. Rape and assault is a violation, not just of a person's body but their entire world. For me, it was not just the act itself, but everything that came after that kept me in a state of limbo. I found it hard to enjoy anything, because emotions, even positive ones, became dangerous; they could open the floodgates.

Ironically, it would be the second of two suicide attempts that saved my life. That day, I turned off my phone so I wouldn't be tempted to call for help, as I had done during the first attempt. I had written a note to my fiancé (a man who really stepped up to the plate in my time of need—a man who showed me how beautiful I am inside and outside, and not the trash I thought I was); I also took off my engagement ring, and even closed the baby gate to keep our dog from interrupting me.

As I began swallowing the pills, I cried out to whomever was listening: "I'm not stopping myself. If I'm meant to live and I'm worthy to live than you better stop me." I don't even know why I said it—by that time I believed I *wasn't* worthy and this was it for me. At least my pain would finally end. Imagine my shock when my fiancé came home much earlier than expected and saw what I was doing. After he had forced water down my throat and after I threw up everything I had taken, he told me he was at work and felt this sudden, powerful need to come home and see me. He felt like he had to leave right then and there, and thank God he did.

Since that day I have fought to live. I encouraged myself to go out and do things—like hike in the mountains with a friend, even though I've never done camping/hiking excursions before. I joined an online support group for victims of rape and assault, and most importantly I continued to see my psychologist (I was cancelling a lot on her before the second attempt). I started to think of my future as one full of possibilities, and that I was worthy of it. Most importantly, I began to realize that what had happened was not my fault. I could not change it, but I did have the power to decide what I was going to do about it.

As part of my healing, I ordered books from Amazon on how to deal with rape, many of which included exercises that helped me free myself of the prison I'd been trapped in. These books helped me to feel comfortable with intimacy again, emotional and physical. To this day I still use some of these tools: I use vision boards and cut out or draw what I want to bring into my life. I write letters to people and though I never share them with those people, I write and read them out loud with my counsellor and burn them with sage. I started a gratitude list and wrote down everything I am thankful for. I have a Divine Box, in which I place my letters to the Divine about everything—including what I'm grateful for and what needs to be let go of. I started to practice yoga again and am proud to say I'm now a certified yoga teacher; I'm also working toward fulfilling my reiki hours so I can join the Canadian Reiki Association. I plan to start a website because I want to share various healing tools with others. And last but not least, I decided to share my story here!

It's been a very long and difficult path, but it has also allowed me to learn so much about myself, about others and about life. There are still days where I am "triggered," yet there are many more successes than setbacks. Each year, I used to mark the "anniversary" of the attack, but in 2016, I didn't. Instead it was a day like any other, and it was a good day! I allowed it to be a good day by focusing not on my pain, but on what I have gained from that experience. I focused on my strengths; I focused on my family,

I focused on my amazing accomplishments, I focused on my vision board, and I focused on forgiveness. Forgiving myself and my rapist were the hardest part of this journey, but they were also the most critical. I had to do it, in order to set myself free.

It is my deepest wish that in sharing this I can help other survivors empower themselves. If you're one of them, just know you are beautiful, worthy, and very much loved. You are *never* alone. Allow this book and others that resonate with your soul to be your spiritual intervention, and remember, sometimes the hardest thing to do is to work through your pain, but it's also the only way to heal. My love to you all. Blessed be.

ABOUT THE AUTHOR: Jessica Tucker is a teacher, writer, and healer passionate about helping people of all ages become the best version of themselves. She has diplomas in Community Social Service Work and Early Childhood Education, and for the past ten years has traveled the world teaching English to children and providing after-school care and daycare. She also teaches infant massage to parents. Jessica is a certified yoga teacher and Reiki II practitioner, and incorporates crystals into her work to better assist her clients in their healing journey. She lives with her family in Calgary.

Jessica Tucker
jessica.tucker133@gmail.com
780-972-0003

The Myth of Arrival
Empowerment through Changing Circumstances
Lucy Vajime

Like many people, I always had the dream of stability, of "arriving" at some circumstance that equaled happiness. Yet, for years, that stability seemed just out of reach. My husband and I met in Tamale, Ghana in 1976, and married after a short courtship. Four years and two kids later, he decided he wanted to return to Nigeria, where he had grown up. Though I didn't want to leave Tamale, I did understand his desire to go back to his home country, so when he was offered a position at Ahmadu Bello University (ABU) I decided to embrace a new adventure. Indeed, life in the university town of Zaria, Kaduna State was as exciting as it was diverse. The staff and student bodies of ABU were a mix of all nationalities, including African, European, and American. There were also a number of amenities: one could socialize, play games, swim, and exercise in any of the three clubs located on the two campuses, Congo and Samaru. As for our own children, there were a number of nursery schools with excellent staff, and a crèche run by some staff members' wives and organizations such as the Nigerian Association of University Women (NAUW).

Still, there was a significant period of adjustment for me. Samaru Village lay just across the university fence, yet it might as well have been a different world. The people there were predominantly Muslim, and it was normal to encounter women clad in hijabs with eye slits so small, one wondered if they could even see through them. It was also very difficult to find reliable domestic help in Zaria, and if one was lucky enough to find someone who would cut the grass, do laundry, or babysit for a couple of hours a day, it hardly lasted more than a month or two. A woman would take a job as a nanny for some desperate family from the university campus, only to quit when she earned enough money to buy the necklace she wanted to wear to the Moslem *Id el Kabir,* or some other upcoming festival. Once she had that money, she would quit, sometimes without even giving notice. For me, this was frustrating as I tried to juggle being a wife and mother with my editing job. It was also a daily reminder of my need to adjust to new circumstances.

Still, the benefits of living in Zaria far outweighed any negatives, which in time I learned to view as insignificant. For the next thirteen years we enjoyed the rich, kaleidoscopic view Zaria afforded us. It was also an excellent place to raise children, and in those years we'd had two more. We had a good life. I thought we were settled. I didn't yet realize that you never know what may be around the bend.

In 1992, my husband was offered another job, this time to start a new university in his home state of Benue. For him, it was the opportunity of a lifetime; for me, it signified complete and utter upheaval. Benue was a nine-hour car ride from Zaria, meaning I would never again be able to drop in on friends or go to my favorite shops. Three of our four children were now grown and thriving in their secondary schools; they had also learnt to speak Hausa, having traded it with the little Twi they had spoken back in Ghana. They too would now have to adjust to a completely new place. Only the youngest, who was barely three years old, would be starting with a clean slate.

In 1992, my husbanded headed off to Makurdi, Benue's state capital and the future location of the new university; the rest of us followed in April 1993. Benue welcomed us with its robust vitality, music, and dance. It also had an extremely humid, hot climate that, compared with Zaria's cold *harmattan* (the windy season from November to March) and dry, hot season, felt like an oppressive blanket. In those early days, I learned much from our children, who quickly adapted to their new environment. Our middle daughter, Iyadoo, immediately fell in love with the Tiv music native to the area. Iyadoo observed that the dance was easy to learn because it was having to balance one's movements. If one swayed to the left, one must also sway to the right in the subsequent movement. Our youngest child could distinguish Tiv music any time she heard it. She said, in her childlike manner, that it was like a mosquito whining.

Our children also adapted to another change, one that would soon sweep the globe. Though computers were still considered a "fad" back then, my husband and I felt that learning basic skills would help our children be adequately prepared for university studies. We enrolled them in computer classes, which they took while on holidays from the secondary school, and bought our own computer so they would have ample opportunity to practice at home. Any doubts we had about their interest level disappeared when we installed a program called Typing Tutor. Soon the three older children were spending hours in the study, competing to see who would be the fastest in typing. I even surprised myself by joining them, and we all loved the music that accompanied the exercises. I found myself blocking off an hour each day to practice on the computer, even if it meant not entertaining people who dropped by for a visit. Before long, I no longer needed a typist to type my papers for publication consideration or my formal letters. When email came along, I learnt from my children how to check it, and my husband's niece, Rita, who was even more computer savvy, created an email address for me. Little by little, I was acclimating to my new home, and taking my place in the digital world as well.

It was around this time that the idea of becoming a coach began to germinate. The thought of being able to help people take the reins of their own lives appealed to me. It also sounded like an excellent next step once I retired from teaching. I could work from the comfort of my home, without the hustle of driving to work or fitting into an employer's schedule. That said, I also knew I would face somewhat of a challenge, maybe even an uphill battle. In Africa, coaching for footballers, athletes, and sportsmen was very common; however, coaching for "regular" individuals was not. Yet to me it made sense. I had been teaching others, in one capacity or another, almost all my life; I could now bring that experience into coaching to empower others to create better versions of themselves, by choice.

I began conservatively, accessing free eBooks and signing up for some free lessons. In 2010, I committed to a paid course—Christy Whitman's Quantum Success Coaching Academy (QSCA)—which advertised that coaching was going to be in high demand in the near future. It wasn't until after I enrolled that I realized just how challenging my new education would be. First, the weekly webinars were held each Thursday from nine to ten p.m. Eastern Standard Time; this meant that I had to be up and at my computer at two or three a.m., depending on the time of year. Attendance was compulsory for all webinars, and if I missed more than two I risked failing the entire course. Second, each student had to practice coaching for free, using volunteer clients arranged by the QSCA. One had to put in a total of ten half-hour coaching sessions, recorded, transcribed, and sent to the QSCA for evaluation. I had a difficult time learning how to record my coaching sessions because by that time my children—who would have gladly taught me—were away at boarding school.

That was when I hit a wall. My time zone diminished my chances of finding willing prospects. Clients had to call me for the session, and not many were willing to pay international fees. My biggest challenge, though, was finding people to transcribe the recorded sessions for the QSCA. Their fees usually ran from fifty to one-hundred dollars, which would have been fine except I was unable to process the payments through PayPal. The resulting delays prevented me from submitting my sessions to the QSCA on time, but when I informed them of the problem, I was given an option to retake the course! I couldn't believe what I was hearing. Frustrated and disheartened, I might have given up on my dream if Linda—a woman from Upstate New York and a colleague in the course—hadn't cared enough to check in with me. When she heard what happened, she kindly offered to pay the transcription fees for me. I was incredibly moved that a complete stranger from the other side of the world, had become my saving grace.

Encouraged by her act of generosity, I decided I would retake the course. In October 2012, I re-registered and began the late-night sessions all over again. With Linda's help, I hired two different transcribers and was able to regularly send my sessions to the QSCA. The following October, I finally received my signed certificate as a Law of Attraction coach from the Quantum Success Coaching Academy.

Even that pivotal moment was not the end of my journey, however; in fact, certification was just the beginning. I now faced the challenging task of finding coaching clients in my own community, or as I called it, "fishing in my own pond." I began organizing speaking engagements and arranging six-week meditation classes to introduce people to life coaching and how it would help them organize their lives better. It has been a long walk, and each step has had its own challenges, setbacks, and victories.

All in all, becoming a coach has been a wonderful, empowering experience. I love teaching others to bring more order, simplicity, and joy to their lives, and helping them realize that they are the architects of their fate and have all they need to build, and rebuild, their lives. Most of all, it has taught me that life is not about stability, but about remaining stable, regardless of changing circumstances.

ABOUT THE AUTHOR: Lucy Irene Vajime is a writer, professor of literature, and Certified Law of Attraction Life Coach. Born and raised in Ghana, she lives with her family in Nigeria, where she has taught for over two decades at Benue State University in Makurdi. Her own experiences and love of teaching inspired her to help others navigating life transitions. In her coaching practice she aspires to empower her clients with processes to manage their lives, rather than allowing the world to manage them.

Lucy Irene Vajime
lifecoachliv.com
livajime@yahoo.com
+234-803-448-7997

Trauma, Temerity, and Tibetan Bowls

How Sound Healing Saved My Life
Barbara Pabisz

Ex Umbris Ad Lucem... When I saw this phrase, meaning "out of the darkness and into the light," it immediately captured my attention. I wrote it down and put it under a Golden Retriever magnet on my fridge, where it stayed for years. At times I would take it down with thoughts of discarding it, only to leave it on the kitchen counter. Later it went back on the fridge, now stained with water and coffee. I thought the phrase resonated because I'd enjoyed taking Latin in school. Little did I know how much it would come to mean to me.

Sometimes, our journey into the light is a conscious one, made up of a series of deliberate decisions; however, when we continue to make choices not in alignment with our potential or true-life purpose, the Universe gets our attention with a "course correction" (otherwise known as a swift kick in the pants).

My own course correction began on a Friday evening in July 2000. I left the veterinary hospital where I worked and headed toward my son's preschool, relieved to put another week behind me. After ten years, I still loved my job, but I couldn't shake the feeling that it was time to move on. Whenever the desire to leave popped up, my mind would step in to remind me of the many practical reasons to stay.

When I saw my son, my stress was immediately replaced with joy. We spent the ride home, singing songs, making up our own words to the standard classics, and generally having a great time. We were within blocks of home when I noticed a minivan coming up very fast behind me. I made the turn at one stop sign, then another, still noting that this minivan was following and seemed to be in quite a hurry. It was as I made the right turn into my driveway that I heard the loud crash. From there, my memory exists only in brief, frightening flashes: the car spinning sideways, then me outside it, freeing my son from his car seat, and finally, sitting on my porch, waiting for the police. That's it. I had no idea that I was about to begin a lengthy education in Traumatic Brain Injury! That night I had numbness on one side of my head, my ear was closed like when you have a bad cold and a sudden onset of vertigo so severe that one second I was sitting at the dinner table and the next I was grabbing onto the edge for dear life. When I began to have trouble speaking, we knew it was time to go to the hospital. At the ER I didn't know the name of my street or the president (though I did recall his wife's name, Hillary), yet they still said I was fine and sent me home! The next morning I still felt the numbness, my ear was still closed, and I just felt kind of, well, weird.

I was dropping things quite a bit, and easily irritated by everyday sounds, which was not like me. My sense of taste was off as well. One night, while out to dinner at a local seafood restaurant, I told my husband that my lobster seemed "bad"! He ate it, no problem, and I chalked it up to another "weird" occurrence.

The following week I was at work when suddenly the sharpest, deepest pain shot from between my shoulder blades up my spine and into my brain. It was so powerful that it sent me to the ground. Until then, I'd always been an extremely physical person—camping, biking, exercising, bowling and horseback riding were all second nature. Scrapes, bruises and pulled muscles had never fazed me. THIS WAS SOMETHING ENTIRELY DIFFERENT!

The doctor said I was having a muscle spasm, wrote me a prescription and sent me on my way. He was wrong. Soon I was having trouble adding and making constant mistakes with the accounts receivable/payable at work. I found myself wandering around, trying to remember what I had just been doing or what I was supposed to be doing. Ultimately I lost my job, which was devastating, and things would only go downhill from there. I had constant chronic pain throughout my head and upper body, intermittent numbness down my arms, and vertigo. Perhaps most disturbing was that now ANY sound, even that of a whisper, would send shooting pain into my neck and brain! I couldn't add or read; everything I looked at appeared to be vibrating; and I had no short-term recall. Light exacerbated the pain, and I spent as much time as possible in the dark.

My journey back began months later, when I started seeing a neuropsychologist. First, he verified that I was not crazy—the accident had caused a closed head concussion! That was the good news. The bad news was that he couldn't tell me how much of my ability to read or recall would return, or if it would at all! I'd have a better idea in approximately twelve months' time. As if that wasn't enough, I also learned I had undiagnosed, chronic Lyme disease.

I tried everything I could think of: chiropractic, acupuncture, kinesiology, trigger point injections, pain medications, and neurological medications. I saw the best neurosurgeons in New York, hoping they could "fix" me. We bought a new mattress, what seemed like a hundred pillows, heating devices, and shoes (yes, what you wear on your feet affects your entire spine!). Still, one doctor informed me that I could easily become a quadriplegic if I fell, was in another accident, or even had a rough landing on a flight! For hours afterward, I drove around in a state of disbelief, but the thought that kept coming to me was *never give up*. I decided then that I never would.

"The body is held together by sound. The presence of disease indicates that some sounds have gone out of tune." ~ Deepak Chopra

Ten years after the accident, I was perusing a site for Golden Retriever lovers when an ad for Sound Healing popped up. Intrigued, I clicked on it. There was a person nearby who used crystal singing bowls for group meditation. I didn't think too much about it— just signed up for a group session.

When I got to there, everyone was lying on yoga mats. Not me, though. I couldn't lie flat and had to use the woman's massage table. It was still painful, but manageable. The sounds were beautiful and my body seemed to soak them in. I was hooked. Each week, I drifted into an increasingly deeper, more peaceful state. Six months later I was told that if I was to continue I'd have to lie on a yoga mat. I was still having trouble sleeping in a bed, so how could I lie on the floor? I thought about how the sound therapy had improved my neuro issues and decreased my pain, then I put my positive intention out there and eased onto the floor. It wasn't easy —I had to shift positions, and I did not go into as deep a state as I had on the massage table—but I did it!

Enter the Tibetan Singing Bowls. The woman had begun using them in private sessions. These particular TSBs were made for brain entrainment. At the very first strike of the bowl something changed in my brain or nervous system or perhaps my entire being. By the hour's end I had experienced a huge shift in my body and energy. More dedicated than ever, I signed up for several private sessions a week, and within a few months I was feeling better more of the time. My dystonic events were becoming more infrequent and I was much happier!

My next step was to learn to play these bowls myself. I signed up for a two-day workshop. The first day was a combination of meditation, seminar, and practice. It was enjoyable yet challenging, and when I returned to my hotel room I was in pain and doubtful that I could make it the next day! As panic set in, I focused on quieting my body, my mind, and then my entire spirit. This in itself brought a major revelation. Until that moment the inability to "focus" on anything had been a daily reminder of my traumatic brain injury, but after just one day of immersion in sound, that was beginning to change. The next day was proof of my progress. I learned a great deal more about the bowls, both from the wonderful instructor and the stories of others in the class. This would have been impossible just four months earlier! It had taken more than a decade, but I was finally able to see the reason for my struggle. I was to bring light and hope to other people who had suffered as I had.

"If you want to know the secrets of the universe, think of Energy, Frequency and Vibration!" ~ Nikola Tesla

As I delved deeper into Sound Healing, I came across the work of Mitchell L. Gaynor, a very progressive, well-known New York Oncologist and Sound Healer. Gaynor wrote:

Sound enters the healing equation from several directions. It may alter cellular functions through energetic effects; it may entrain biological systems to function more homeostatically; it may calm the mind and therefore the body; or it may have emotional effects, which influence neurotransmitters and neuropeptides, which in turn help to regulate the immune system—the healer within.

I can personally attest to the truth of this—not only for myself, but others as well.

A home health aide I know told me about her neighbor, a forty-two-year-old woman, "Diane," diagnosed with terminal cancer. The aide was certain Sound Healing could help. I told her it was important that Diane want to be helped and that she should reach out to me. When we met I observed a woman with a quiet demeanor, extremely low energy/vibration, and a lack of joy. She also had a pale complexion and was obviously in pain as she limped into the room. After speaking about her current condition and symptoms, we began. At the very first strike of the bowl her foot began to move slowly up then down and continued to do so for the entire session. Her head and fingers twitched and jerked, all on the side of the body where she'd had skin grafts and nerve damage and a tumor removed. It is not unusual for the body to show signs of release during a session, often without the person realizing it. When I asked Diane if she felt her foot moving, she looked a bit surprised. She had no feeling in that foot, a little fact she'd forgotten to mention earlier! She walked into her second session with MUCH improved energy and a big smile. It was as if her true self had woken up. I knew just how she felt. During the fourth session, she heard a *whoosh* in her deaf ear—the first sound since her surgery. She also laughed a lot more and had an amazing glow about her. What a difference since our first meeting! I wasn't the only one who noticed—she said several people had commented on how great she looked and asked what she was doing! THAT is the power of Sound and Vibrational Healing.

Treatment with Sound Healing will empower you and can help change your life. It encompasses the mind, body, and spirit and played a pivotal part of my "course correction." I am now doing what I was meant to do: bring hope to those who have forgotten what hope is. After their first session, clients often say, "Wow, that was hard to describe." I just smile and nod. It is hard to put into words, but it's nothing less than a miracle.

Ex Umbris Ad Lucem!

ABOUT THE AUTHOR: Barbara is a Certified Master Sound Healer & Teacher, Biofield Practitioner, Reiki Master Teacher, retired Certified Equine Sports Massage Therapist and passionate animal lover. A born intuitive, she recalls practicing energy healing on her pets at the age of five. Her gifts of clairvoyance, clairsentience, and clairaudience were exponentially heightened after suffering a traumatic brain injury from a car accident. After years of chronic pain and cognitive problems, Barbara was Divinely guided to Sound Healing, which dramatically improved her health and led her to help others. Today Barbara offers sound healing and meditation sessions for individuals and groups. She belongs to the International Academy of Sound Healing, Sound Healers Association and Reiki Membership Association.

Barbara Pabisz
im4sound.com
im4sound@gmail.com

Being My True Self
Danielle Dawn Hayes

To a kid, there is nothing worse than being labeled weird. It's like being condemned to a life of isolation and loneliness, because who would want to hang out with a weird person? It also becomes a self-fulfilling prophecy, at least it did for me. As a result of being called weird, I became quite shy, making it even more difficult to connect with other kids. Soon, I was being singled out for being different and even "stuck up." This was ironic, since it was shyness, not arrogance, that made me standoffish. By the time I got to high school I was desperate to find a place where I felt comfortable and safe being me. As you can imagine, this played out in many unhealthy ways and made it difficult for me to navigate the world. I even thought about working at the suicide hotline so I could help others like me.

It was a book that helped me turn things around. I was a voracious reader and interested in a wide variety of topics. One day I came upon *Sybil,* the famous book about a woman who endured horrific abuse as a child and developed Multiple Personality Disorder (now known as Dissociative Identity Disorder). As I was drawn into Sybil's world, I became fascinated by the capabilities of the human mind. I began studying more about Multiple Personality Disorder and while still in high school wrote reports and gave speeches on it. I wanted to learn as much as I could about human resilience—in particular, why some people survive when others in similar situations do not.

This discovery also gave me a direction in which to channel my desire to help people. I had no real models for this type of work. It was not valued in my small, rural community; psychology classes were not even offered at my high school. Though I wasn't sure how I would go about it, I knew I wanted to spend my life studying what makes people tick.

Then the doubts started creeping in. No one in my life saw any value in getting a psychology degree. I heard things like, "Oh honey, you can't make any money in psychology," and "You want to make sure you can support yourself." Though these statements and others came from a place of deep love and caring, they did little for my confidence. When the time came to start college, I chose a major I was told would lead to a lucrative career: Engineering. I am also good at math, so on some level it did make sense to me. Still, there was a part of me that was not willing to let go of my dream. I minored in Psychology, and when the time came to declare a specific discipline of engineering to major in, I chose Industrial Engineering, which is basically the management of people. I can look back now and see that the desire to learn psychology and help people was still trying to come through. I just didn't know how to listen to that part of me. It was only a matter of time before I was forced to listen.

At first I did well in college, but by Junior year, when I got into actual engineering classes, I started to struggle. Of course I did, because I had no passion for them. I failed a couple of classes or dropped them because I was on the verge of failing. Still, I was determined to stay the course, otherwise it would mean *I* was a failure. Now, as I have come to understand the ways of the universe, something had to give, either by purposeful choice or by divine intervention. Mine went the way of the latter; I got pregnant. Though I was single and it was not planned, I knew immediately that I was going to keep the baby. As scared and freaked out as I was, I was also relieved because it meant that I got to leave engineering and college without having "failed." Mind you, this is all hindsight. At the time I just felt a conviction to do what I did. It resonated with something deep inside me.

My focus became all about my new baby and providing for her. I felt like we were a team and I was excited for our future. Shortly after she was born I met a man and we started dating. I was relieved to find someone that was actually interested in me, as I had been told repeatedly that single mothers are unattractive and unappealing. I had also been cheated on before and felt lucky that

I'd found someone who would be loyal. I was so focused on these things, though, that I missed (or dismissed) some pretty serious red flags. In marrying him, I was once again listening to all the voices around me, saying this was the responsible thing to do, rather than my own voice, which knew it wasn't right.

I had three more children (including a set of twins), for which I am immensely grateful, and spent several years as a stay-at-home mom. I was delighted to be able to do this and it simply made financial sense at the time. I volunteered at my church and the kids' parochial school, yet at the same time, I knew I was not cut out to be the cookie-making mom. As they got older I began to think seriously about returning to college. It was about this time that my marriage ended. I do not believe in regrets and I wouldn't change a thing; in fact, I am thankful for those years, although they were some of the toughest of my entire life. It wasn't until I left, however, that I realized just how much of myself I had lost. I had to find a way back to the stuff that made me, *me*.

And so, after moving out and establishing a residence for myself and the kids, I enrolled at a branch of the same university I had attended years earlier. Though I was only taking one sociology class, I was excited and nervous. Would I be able to do it? Who was I to start over after all this time? That's when I found a quote that struck me to the core of my being: "Well behaved women rarely make history." It became my motto. I had been put down, ridiculed, and dismissed most of my life. I had done everything up to this point according to someone else's plans and ideas. I wasn't going to do that anymore. It was like I was a rubber band, snapping in the other direction, and nothing and no one was going to stop me.

In just two years (thanks to all those engineering prep classes) and while raising four children ages four to eleven, I had completed my Bachelor of Science in Psychology. I wasn't done though. After briefly considering a PhD, I decided that a master's degree in Counseling would be a better fit, as it would allow me to do most of what I wanted to do in half the time.

While still an undergrad I had applied for this program and was granted an interview. Imagine my surprise when I walked in and found it was a group interview! I left there convinced I would not get in and even began thinking about a Plan B. Several weeks later, I received an even greater shock—a phone call letting me know that out of more than one hundred applicants, I was one of the fifteen chosen for the program!

Two years later, I graduated with a master's degree in Mental Health Counseling. After six months of searching, I got my first counseling job at a community mental health center. It was hard work. We were expected to meet certain productivity numbers each month. We were also on call for the local hospital all day, every day for mental health crises. I did that for a little over four years, and by the time it was over, I was burned out. I even started to wonder if I had made a mistake with my chosen field.

Rather than throw it all out, I decided to make a small change. I joined an established private group practice. After two years, I was ready for another shift, this time to my own private practice. While getting that up and running, I made ends meet by teaching at a small nursing school and working part time at Home Depot. Before I knew it, I had left those jobs and was seeing clients fulltime.

As gratifying as this was, I still felt there was something else I was called to do. I spent all my continuing education time learning about alternative healthcare and incorporated these things into my practice as much as I could. This earned me the reputation as the town "witch doctor"! Yet again, I was struggling to fit in, so I decided to move my practice.

That was two years ago. Since then, I have certainly found more of my people, my tribe, both locally and all over the world. I do have the lingering feeling that I have not quite arrived at my real mission, but I have embraced that feeling and remain determined to search until I find it. More importantly, I have come to embrace what I have always known: that I'm different than most everyone around me. I am who I am today because of the life experiences I've had. I am proud of my decision to make my kids my priority, and of the fact that I worked hard to provide for them while at the same time pursuing my soul's desire. The kids have become wonderful adult human beings and I am truly blessed to have been chosen to be their mother. That will never change. Now, however, is my time to truly stretch my wings and follow my soul's yearnings, confident that the kids are well on their way to living their own fulfilling lives.

Now, as I prepare to embark on the next chapter of my life, I find myself filled with youthful anticipation. I do not know exactly what this chapter looks like, but that is the best part! If I tried to create what I am yearning for, I would be limited by my own imagination. Instead, I am opening with abandon to the magnitude of possibilities the world has to offer. I do know that it will include travel and a warm place to live. It will also include nutrition and wellness—as I have discovered this is a cornerstone of a healthy, empowered life—and life coaching, as this is my passion. Seeing my clients discover the strength, power, and confidence to live their truth, regardless of what those around them say, is beautiful. If I honor that which is in me and you do the same, a wonderful symbiotic relationship is created, one that is mutually respectful and supportive, by and for all.

ABOUT THE AUTHOR: Danielle Dawn Hayes is a Transformation Coach who incorporates health and wellness techniques for a truly unique approach to empowerment. She holds a B.S. in Psychology and a M.Ed. in Counseling from Ohio State University, where she was an award-winning student and published academic author. Danielle is currently writing a book about finding her soul's path, and is developing a program to help others do the same. Forever the non-conformist, after living her entire life in Ohio, she has picked up stakes and is travelling in search of new horizons while continuing to work with clients virtually and over the phone.

Danielle Dawn Hayes
Being My True Self
danielledawnhayes.com
danielledawnhayes@gmail.com
Blog: beingmytrueself.com

Empowering the Light Within
Roseanne Dawes

I am a light. That's right, a light. You know when you see a newborn baby; that pure glow about them? They have an almost angelic look about them, as if they were sent right from heaven. This light draws people in, makes them smile, and is an instant energy-booster. Babies tug on the heartstrings and give the rest of us hope for the future.

I believe that as a baby, I came into this world feeling completely safe. This safety came with an understanding that I was perfect! I felt valued, loved, accepted, and that I could do no wrong. Then little by little, experiences in life, just normal every day experiences, would affect my thinking patterns. I learned through these experiences that there are certain situations that were not safe, that I could do things that others did not approve of; they challenged my sense of self-worth and value. I no longer thought of myself as a perfect being. Before I knew it, these thoughts had become patterns of insecurity and self-blame that showed up in my life as addiction.

By the time I was five years old, I knew I was bigger than most of the children in kindergarten or in my dance class. By the time I was twelve, I knew that food was a source of comfort for me. By the spring of my junior year in high school, I had started my first real diet. After losing forty-five pounds, I learned that when I was thin, I felt more accepted by people. Boys actually wanted to date me. Then came my twenties and four beautiful babies that enriched my life and wreaked havoc on my figure. During each pregnancy I would gain anywhere from sixty to one hundred pounds, then find myself on another diet after giving birth. I didn't like myself heavy. I didn't feel my worth as a "chunky mom." With all the negative dialogue inside my head, I noticed that my light was getting dimmer and dimmer…and sometimes it would even be turned off.

It wasn't until I was well in my thirties and a chronic yo-yo dieter that I began to understand the connection between my feelings and my eating habits. Dieting and negative thoughts about myself seemed to be my norm. I was either on a diet and losing or off a diet and eating out of control. Once, I lost ninety pounds by restricting my food intake and excessive exercising (and looking really good, by the way) only to begin a cycle of binging once again. The real problem was not an addiction to food, but to my negative thinking patterns. I could always find something about me, or my body, that I did not like.

This epiphany led to a decision that was quite radical, given my history. I would stop dieting until I found a program that would not only help me lose the unhealthy weight, but the unhealthy mind and negative thinking patterns as well. I knew that once I changed my thoughts, it would be that much easier to keep the weight off. Until that happened, however, I would just continue tormenting myself with the vicious cycle of denial, overindulgence, and cruel self-talk. It was time to get off the roller coaster once and for all. I found myself excited to start this journey and finally become the person I knew was inside me.

When the right program did come along, I knew it immediately. I found myself scared and doubting the day I started because I was afraid of another "fail," but I knew I was led to this particular program for a reason. It was exactly what I needed. After a full year of working on my mindset—and losing 136 pounds—I started to notice my glow, my light, come back into my life. I felt so good. I even began sharing the program with others and helping them to become healthier versions of themselves. I knew that my body was happy when my blood sugar was balanced. All I had to do was remember to eat protein/carbohydrate-balanced meals every two or three hours and the cravings and temptations all but vanished! If a craving did start to rear its ugly head, I knew it was just time to balance my blood sugar. I also learned the importance of water and sleep and other healthy physical habits that would ensure my success. The program was that simple!

After coaching clients for about a year, I began to recognize some negative thinking patterns that would keep them from sticking to the plan. I couldn't understand it because I had stuck to the plan perfectly for 365 days. It didn't make sense. Finally, I decided that I needed to "go off plan" and experience what they were experiencing. It didn't take me long to realize that had been a very bad choice. The binge eating was back in full force, a clear indicator that I needed more work. I was, once again, given the perfect opportunity to find out what the emotions and thoughts and feelings were behind the binges. Boy, was I ever so grateful I had learned energy healing modalities along the way, and also neurologically coached by professionals that could help me through this process.

I soon found myself counting my blessings, both for the opportunity to discover the missing aspects of my health program and for having the tools and resources to help me make it even better. THIS is what my program is all about—finding out what else is needed and taking transformative steps. Can I help you release unhealthy weight? Yes! Can I help you do it while learning to keep a healthy mindset? You bet! Can I also help you to increase your financial abundance and make more of you than you ever thought possible? Yes I can! Why? Because I have worked with clients all over the United States, teaching them the importance of the balance of all three. I have the experience, the successes, and the know-how to help you start living a life full of light and joy! Doesn't that sound exciting?

This personal "detour" has also taught me several invaluable lessons. First, I learned that being at one's goal weight is just that, a goal; it is not the only measure of progress or success. I no longer have the attitude of "do what it takes to get the weight off fast"; instead, it's a healthy mindset of loving and honoring my body all while practicing the tools and techniques that will help me keep it off for the long haul. It's an exciting and peaceful journey—one that continues to help my light shine more bright within me.

My second lesson was that I had another life-long pattern: when my eating was off, my spending was off as well. When my eating was on, so was my spending. Clearly there was some connection, not only between my thoughts and my eating habits, but to my finances as well! Once I started to see the significance of keeping all three areas in check, things really started to fall into place. My husband and I were able to pay off all our credit card debt, car loans and student loans; we were even able to take the whole family to Hawaii without charging a cent! Balance in all three areas was becoming my new normal, and my light was starting to shine even more brightly.

As I mentioned earlier, during this time of self-discovery, I had also started studying BodyTalk and energy medicine. At first I was skeptical (in fact, I thought it was crazy!), yet at the same time, I was driven to learn more and more. I noticed that my attitude toward food was transforming. I felt more stable emotionally, and I knew in my heart that I needed to help people who might be suffering with some of the same issues I had faced in my life. Eventually, I resigned my position as an elementary school teacher and became a full-time health coach and Certified BodyTalk/Body Code/Emotion Code Practitioner. I also studied many other energy healing modalities. I just can't seem to get enough of it!

As I continued my education in healing modalities, I noticed that the perfect classes I needed to help my clients became available in exactly the right time. I also noticed that I always had the money to pay for it. Why was this? Because my thoughts and energy towards money and pursuing the desires of my heart were in sync. They were working together for my good. I could feel it, and it was happening all the time!

Learning to follow my heart was not easy. I had become accustomed to "going with the flow," and just taking whatever life handed me. None of it was done with intention, and I was not creating the things I wanted most in life. I didn't even know I needed to do that, let alone know *how* to do it. This realization marked the beginning of a huge shift in my life. I learned I did not have to settle for mediocrity; I could be the author of my story, and attract the things I really wanted. I was an entrepreneur at heart and I had no idea!

Setting intentions and eliminating expectations has become a natural part of my everyday life. I have become proficient at recognizing the worry, doubt, and fear that creep into my thought processes, even when they are subtle and sneaky. More importantly, I have learned the craft of shifting them to "above the line" thinking that ensures a positive, vibrant frequency in which miracles happen in my life every day. THAT is what I share with my clients!

Today, I am blessed to understand that every single struggle, challenge, or difficult situation is exactly what I need to become the best version of myself and create my life. Everything is perfectly handed to me. The trick is to find out what the lesson is in each of them. It's not really a trick; it's a skill that I have become proficient at and now I teach others to do it for themselves. I'm a teacher at heart, and have combined those skills with my entrepreneurial mindset to develop a modality for those whose light has dimmed or completely gone out. I take each client through a series of classes with concepts, ideas, specific thought patterns, brain integration, and other tools that build upon each other to ensure joy in every step of the journey. The important thing for me is to balance a person's body, mind, and finances, and everything else seems to fall right into place. When this happens, the light in my client's eyes begins to shine through. Their excitement for life grows exponentially because they are now empowered with the tools and experiences to chart their own course, in every aspect of life, for the rest of their lives! It truly is a beautiful process.

Sometimes I cannot believe how much my own life has changed. In fact, if someone had told me a few years ago that I would leave my teaching job and be helping others transform, I would have told them they were crazy! But God knew exactly what I needed to be able to be in this place. My trials have been my greatest blessings. They have helped me discover that I DO have desires and passions and that it's not just okay to pursue them, but imperative. In the process I have discovered the real Roseanne, and my purpose: to help empower others so their light can burn bright once again. Even those who have never experienced their light begin to feel it ignite and grow within them.

ABOUT THE AUTHOR: Roseanne Dawes is a health and life coach dedicated to helping her clients see the beauty in the world and achieve balance in their lives. She holds a master's degree in Elementary Education with an emphasis in Music, is certified in several energy healing modalities, and has a wealth of life experiences, all of which she incorporates into her practice to create a unique healing experience for each person seeking her assistance. Aside from her husband, four children, and two beautiful grandchildren, Roseanne's greatest joy is looking at the possibilities life has to offer and receiving inspired ideas to make things happen.

Roseanne Dawes
Here's To Healthy Living
iamroseanne.com
herestohealthyliving@gmail.com
435-749-1433

Wrecked to Fulfilled

My Journey of Empowerment
Cindy Chipchase

"Why did you have to wreck everything?"

Those words, spoken softly by my eight-year-old granddaughter as she lay snuggled next to me, seemed to stop my heart, and my world. They would also begin my fifteen-year journey from feeling "wrecked" to fulfilled and empowered.

I would say I had a pretty average childhood, my days taken up with schoolwork and friends and Barbie Dolls. Then, at the age of twelve, everything seemed to change overnight. My body rapidly transitioned from that of a young girl to a woman, a change I was very unhappy about. Yet at the same time I was no longer content with my friendships, Barbies, and other "childish" stuff. I became interested in the opposite sex and, because I looked older than my age, I attracted their attention as well. By the time I was thirteen, partying, alcohol, and boys were a regular part of my life, and I was ill-equipped to handle it.

My first boyfriend was a charming sixteen-year-old who I was so "in love" with I did not acknowledge or even realize that he had sexually assaulted me until I was in my forties. At a New Year's Eve party, I ended up alone in a bedroom with him. When I cried and asked him to stop, he replied, "I love you, and if you love me, you will have sex with me." There was always a part of me that knew this was wrong, but it took nearly a year and many more *I love yous* before I left the relationship. Fortunately, around this time I also met the boy who would later become my husband.

A few months shy of my fifteenth birthday my world was rocked again when I became pregnant by my eighteen-year-old boyfriend. My mother and grandmother insisted I have an abortion, and though we were in love and wanted to keep our baby, we were also young, scared, and felt we had no say in the decision.

Shortly after the abortion I became pregnant again, and as shocked I was, I was also determined to go through with the pregnancy. Very ill and unable to go to school, I lost all my friends and relied heavily on my family and my boyfriend. Imagine our shock when after my daughter's "premature" birth the doctors realized I had been carrying twins all along; only one was taken in the abortion procedure.

Some might wonder how my parents handled all of this so well. It was because they had lived it before. My mother was just fifteen when she became pregnant with me, and my father turned eighteen the day they were married. Now, at sixteen and eighteen, respectively, my boyfriend and I were also newlyweds, and kids raising a kid. Shortly after our wedding, my parents announced they were separating. It would be the first of three times.

Shame, guilt, fear, and embarrassment over my teenage experiences were so deeply imbedded in my being, so much a part of me, that I did not always recognize them or how they presented in my life. The occasional offhanded comment or conversation would bring them to the surface and send a wave of embarrassment washing over me. I became very good at avoiding conversations about age and/or education, as they made me feel insecure, judged, and not good enough. These feelings set the stage for my subconscious need to please and to settle for less than I desired.

When I was eighteen, my second daughter was born. We lived in a remote area, and other than my husband, my mom was my best and only friend. I was happy with my little family, yet there was always an underlying sense of something missing, a faint sense of longing for something that I did not understand. When my younger daughter was three we moved one hundred miles away, which was both scary and exciting. As much as I missed Mom, I felt like for the first time, my husband and I were truly on our own. I took another big step into adulthood when he suddenly found himself unemployed, and I took a job—my first—as a waitress. I discovered I loved working around and with others, yet neither this job, nor the many that would come later, left me feeling truly fulfilled. It would take years for me to realize that my lack of confidence always held me back from being and doing more, even when the opportunities presented themselves.

By my tenth wedding anniversary, these feelings of longing and emptiness had all but consumed my life. For nine months, I left my daughters with my husband and went in search of what was "missing"; I was in search of myself. During the day I went to school to obtain my high school diploma and at night I worked at a bar. Yet being without my family just made my heart heavy. I returned home and settled back into my life as wife and mother; we adopted our beautiful son and I got a great job as an aide to a special needs student. My life felt pretty complete…for a while.

Through the ups and downs of the past several years, I had started to realize a desire within me to help people. Yet every time I thought I might become a teacher or enter some other profession, the negative self-talk would begin, telling me all the reasons I couldn't and shouldn't follow my dreams; it kept me feeling "less than." Despite this, opportunities to explore and be more continued to show up in my life, and finally resulted in a job as a Training Coordinator.

My new career fed my passion for teaching and helping others; it also required a lot of travel. I knew my husband and I were growing apart again, but that underlying longing, the sense of something missing, kept popping up, telling me I needed to be on my own again. I found myself saying, "We have nothing in common anymore" and "I'm just not "in love" with him anymore." The inner chatter, which I continued to ignore, was working overtime: *Why can't I just be happy with the way things are? What is wrong with me? Why does my body hurt all the time?* After our son graduated, I left my marriage for the second time.

I felt stuck in a state of sadness that I did not know how to climb out of. It would be my granddaughter's haunting words— "Why did you have to wreck everything, Grandma?" —that initiated my first true journey within, to look at my choices and decisions that had shaped my life up to that point.

Repairing my marriage was a raw and tender journey. For the first time my husband and I shared our pain over the abortion, and the many challenges and struggles of our relationship. In the process we reclaimed and rekindled our deep love for one another; we also realized this love is a gift, one that requires our conscious awareness, nurturing, and honoring of each other. Though we still have occasional struggles, we continue to grow and evolve each day.

The sense of contentment I now felt with my life was marred by a diagnosis of Fibromyalgia and a significant back injury. Powerless and depressed, I was desperate to find a way to break the cycle of pain and get off the medication. That's when I discovered Reiki. From my first class, I felt myself connecting with a powerful energy. Within three months my pain had decreased dramatically and I cancelled my appointment with the back surgeon. Finding Reiki led me to an amazing group of women who not only supported me on my healing journey but also encouraged me to help others, to believe in myself and my ability to step into the role of healer and teacher. Reiki helped me find what I felt had been "missing" most of my life, a relationship with Creator, a knowing that I am the essence of love. I have learned to love myself and no longer look to others to fulfill the longing or find the part of me that was missing. Yoga has also helped me strengthen and heal my body and my Spirit, and a deep sense of peace surrounds me when I come to my mat, either as a student or teacher.

Through meditation, prayer, and the loving support of others I have been able to forgive myself, my mother, and grandmother, and even the boy who sexually assaulted me all those years ago. I have come to an understanding and knowing that those experiences are not me, they no longer define me, and they are only things that happened to me. I am learning to understand and appreciate the lessons and gifts woven through them. As part of my process, I have placed these experiences in an imaginary book, which I can access and share with other women without shame, embarrassment, or guilt. I have recently shared my story with my family, feeling the relief and weight of the secrecy fall away. In embracing vulnerability, I feel my inner strength growing and the grip of shame, guilt and fear weaken.

Owning my story and feeling proud of who and where I am in my life has given me a new freedom to move forward. I feel as though my purpose is no longer hidden behind a veil of painful emotions. A new sense of empowerment is filling my soul, and the need for approval from others is melting away as well. A sense of excitement dances within me as I step into and embrace my new way of being. For the past several years I have chosen a "theme word" that I choose to focus on and to represent my year. This year I have chosen "flow." Instead of pressing against, resisting, or trying to make things happen, it is my intention instead to be in the flow and allow for an unfolding, for the Universe to guide me, and to trust myself more. Already, amazing opportunities and synchronicities are unfolding, being an author in this book being only one of them! My deep passion and purpose is to support, uplift, and encourage women on their journey of healing, of forgiveness, of acceptance, and of loving themselves freely and unconditionally.

There are still struggles, big and small, that I face on a regular basis, but my "tools" of meditation, yoga, Reiki, strong family ties, and an amazing sisterhood of women help me remain detached from outcomes and trust that "this too shall pass." A sense of deep peace fills my soul, and I'm learning every day to pay attention to my soul as it speaks to me, often in whispers and heard only in the stillness.

ABOUT THE AUTHOR: Cindy Chipchase is a Reiki Master, Yoga Teacher, Certified Life Coach, and Founder of the Circle of Hearts Society for Women—Connecting and Supporting Women of the North, a society that focuses on heart-centered connection, support, and empowerment of women. Her passion for empowering women evolved from her own healing journey facilitated by Reiki, Yoga, and the support of a strong "Tribe" of women who embraced and supported her. Cindy lives in the geographical center of beautiful British Columbia, Canada with her loving husband of forty-five years. They have three amazing adult children, grandchildren, and great-grandchildren, as well as three dogs.

Cindy Chipchase
Loving Yourself Freely Life Coaching
lovingyourselffreely.com
cindy@lovingyourselffreely.com
250-567-0219

Quarters from Heaven
Jen Silva

We've all heard the saying, "God works in mysterious ways," even when we are faced with a challenging situation or when we feel completely isolated. Perhaps, it's more accurate to say that "God works in mysterious and *subtle* ways." We are always connected to God (or the Universe or whatever you call "Source") often receiving messages from Him, and though sometimes we have to pay close attention, when we do, we find them. It's very empowering to know that I already have all the answers I need and that whatever happens in life, the Universe is *for* me and *guiding* me every step of the way. My own journey to noticing God's messages began with the Law of Attraction.

I first learned about the Law of Attraction—and its connection to our own intuition—while training to be a Life Coach. The truth was, the Law of Attraction had always intrigued me but at the same time I found its principles confusing. Then a friend of mine gave me a book that explained it in a practical, easy-to-understand format and provided exercises to help with manifesting what I wanted. My first assignment was to manifest parking spots. I practiced all the time—at supermarkets, at the mall, and (the real test) in New York City, where parking spots are very hard to find. I was shocked to find it worked every time! It made me excited to try my next attraction assignment, which was about money. I wanted to attract more money into my life but it seemed too big and out of reach. The book recommended starting with smaller, more achievable goals, so I started with coins. To make it more exciting but still believable, I focused on finding quarters, which are less common than pennies. Following the visualization exercise, I pictured quarters in my mind, I felt quarters, told myself I deserved them, and even invited them into my life!

It seemed so ridiculous to do this, but my gut told me to go with it and see what happens. The Law of Attraction is about opening our minds to the different possibilities of how our desires will show up. Within a few days of practicing, I found three quarters on my back porch underneath a pair of my kid's muddy sneakers! Suddenly, I was finding quarters all the time; on the street, in my pockets, in my handbag, even in the laundry. The Law of Attraction was working! What I didn't yet realize was that these quarters were about to mean a lot more to me than just manifesting more money into my life. They were about to be put in my path, literally and spiritually, to show me that God is always listening.

"It's going to happen to me, I just know it, it's inevitable." This was the message I'd been telling myself since I was twenty-one years old. By that time, both of my parents had passed away from cancer and I was terrified of getting this terrible disease. Every year, when it came time for my mammogram and MRI, I was overwhelmed with fear. It takes a lot of work to keep calm and trust that all is okay. *"It's only a routine mammogram and ultrasound,"* I told myself. I repeated it over and over again even when the radiologist saw something and wanted to do more tests. What was it? What does she see? Then I heard those awful words: "There's something there and we should do a biopsy." Suddenly it was difficult to breathe.

This is it. I have cancer. What am I going to do?

I walked outside where the sun was shining bright and got into my car and cried. It was a day to be happy and grateful and enjoying life—not to be fearful of it.

To get some fresh air and to try to calm down, I got out and walked aimlessly in the parking lot alone. Fear came over me, as it always did, but somewhere underneath it I felt a sense of calm. A still, small voice inside whispered, "Everything is okay." I desperately wanted to trust this feeling but didn't know how. I just wanted someone to tell me I was okay. Walking around, I started praying and asked God to "show" me that everything was alright. I wanted a clear, concrete sign that I could trust this voice. It's not typically how God works but I asked for an absolute message anyway. In that moment of prayer, I looked down and there in the middle of that big, empty parking lot was my sign—a quarter! *My quarter.* My message directly from God that I could trust my gut and I would be okay. I froze. I picked it up to make sure it was real. Just then, ego crept in and told me it was just a silly coincidence. I challenged my ego and walked the whole parking lot in search of other coins. There was not one other coin in that whole lot! Not one penny, nickel, or dime. When the shock subsided, I was overwhelmed with a feeling of gratitude. This was my message from God that I needed to trust my intuition that I was going to be fine. I kept that quarter in my jewelry box as a reminder that God sends us messages and it was up to me to pay attention to them, but most of all, to trust them. My intuition and my message were right; I did not have cancer. It was a stubborn cyst that needed to be removed.

I'm a runner. Running is my time to take care of not only my physical well-being but also my mental and spiritual fitness too. While I run, I talk to God about whatever is on my mind. Praying while I run brings me the clarity and peace of mind that I need at times when I just don't have the answers. Somehow, some way, the answers just seem to come together through prayer. Very often, though, my "head" gets in the way and I don't trust the answers that come. I question, I overthink, I tell myself stories that are completely untrue, anything to keep me from trusting Life. I often practice trusting and letting go but I guess the Universe knows when I'm kind of full of it!

Not too long after finding my special quarter, I was on an early morning run in the rain. My emotions were running high, I remember, because I was in a relationship that I knew on some level wasn't best for me. I couldn't put my finger on anything specific, other than it just didn't feel quite right. Dismissing this feeling seemed much easier than going deeper to see what was there. Maybe I was too scared of what I would find, for if there was a reason to validate my feelings I would have to make a tough decision and leave the relationship. So, my indecision was my decision.

As time moved on, it became clear that denial was no longer working. That uneasy feeling was still plaguing me, and I finally had to ask myself those questions that I'd always been afraid to ask. Those simple, honest, difficult questions like: Is this relationship best for me? Am I at my best with this person? Does this relationship bring out the best in both of us? I had to have the courage to face the answers and deep down, I already had them.

Ego has a way of standing in our way, blocking us from what we're really feeling. Oftentimes, ego is about fear. Fear of following what our hearts know for sure, fear of paying attention to what's right for us, fear of admitting to ourselves what we really want. Deep down I knew my truth but I quickly dismissed it. Instead, my ego stepped in and gave me reasons why this relationship was still working. So, I stayed. He treated me well, and though I wasn't getting what I really needed, I pretended it was enough. It's funny how life works sometimes. We can fool ourselves but we can't fool the Universe.

Eventually, the relationship ended…and it was messy. Playing the victim for a long time, I blamed him for all of it. Then one morning, on my early run, I did a lot of soul-searching about it, about him, and about us. Again, I asked myself the tough questions: is any of this a surprise? Didn't I see this coming? Looking back, doesn't it make sense now? Then I remembered…from very early in the relationship I'd known deep down that it just wasn't right for me. There was always something telling me he wasn't the one. I knew this at my core, but I chose not to listen. At that exact moment, I looked down and there on the street was a quarter! It was as if God had heard my thoughts and said, "Yes!" I smiled to myself and picked it up while thanking God out loud for confirming, once again, that my intuition was right and for sending me a clear message.

God is always sending us messages and sometimes in mysterious ways. He always knows what's best for us. It is up to us to open our hearts and our minds to the infinite number of ways He chooses to communicate with us. We might see a message on a bumper sticker or on TV, or hear it on the radio or during a conversation with a friend. It can even present itself as a feeling we have about something. It's our intuition however, that serves as our greatest messenger. It usually comes in a small, still voice, even a whisper, when trying to get our attention. We need only take a moment from our busy lives and really listen.

I choose to believe that my personal "signs" are the many quarters and other coins that I find in various places. What's exciting is these coins don't only just show up in response to a prayer. There have been times when I find quarters out of the blue and in the most random places. Whenever and wherever I find them, I'm in a place of such gratitude and awe. I simply smile and thank God, for I feel on a very deep level that He's simply telling me I am on the right path and living my truth.

And what about that very first quarter that let me know I was cancer-free? That, I had made into a pendant and wear it as a reminder to simply *TRUST LIFE. What an empowering feeling!*

ABOUT THE AUTHOR: Jen Silva, CEC, ELI-MP, is an Empowerment Coach and graduate of the Institute for Professional Excellence in Coaching. Even with the growth of gender diversity in the workplace, Jennifer believes women are still held back from advancing in their careers relative to their male counterparts. One reason for this is the core thoughts and limiting beliefs that many women hold about themselves. Jen's unique approach facilitates a dramatic shift in each's woman's perspective about who she is and what she can accomplish, allowing her to step into her personal power and become a more effective, dynamic leader.

Jen Silva
Jennifer Silva Coaching
Jennifersilvacoaching@gmail.com
908-752-5287

About the Authors

**Are you inspired by the stories in this book?
Let the authors know.**

**See the contact information at the end of each chapter
and reach out to them.**

They'd love to hear from you!

Author Rights & Disclaimer

Each author in this book retains the copyright and all inherent rights to their individual chapter. Their stories are printed herein with each author's permission.

Each author is responsible for the individual opinions expressed through their words. Powerful You! Publishing bears no responsibility for the content of the stories by these authors.

Acknowledgements & Gratitude

OUR GRATITUDE overflows to the many incredible women who have come together with such open hearts to lift the world, one woman at a time, to a space of joy, love, possibility, and empowerment.

There are many beautiful souls who we gratefully call our tribe who offer their guidance, expertise, love, and support!

To the authors of these stories we applaud you, honor you, and love you. You exemplify resilience, courage, selflessness and, even more than these, you radiate pure love and the beauty of the human spirit. We are honored to share this journey with you, and so grateful that you stepped fully into your power by offering your own story to light the way for others. You are a beautiful example of love in action.

Our editor Dana Micheli who knows the deep questions to ask to get to the heart and essence of the stories. We are so very grateful for you.

Our awesome training team, AmondaRose Igoe, Kathy Sipple, and Linda Albright—your caring hearts and vast expertise light the way for our new authors. We love and appreciate each of you!

Dr. Jo Anne White, dear friend and enlightened spirit—your words are a masterpiece of inspired truth to light the way for our authors to shine.

Our friends and families, we love you! Your unwavering and loving support of our inspirations and projects continue to allow us to faithfully pursue our passion and vision for life.

Above all, we are grateful for the Divine Spirit that flows through us each day providing continued blessings, lessons, and opportunities for growth, peace, and JOY!

Namaste` and Blessings
with much love and deep gratitude,
Sue Urda and Kathy Fyler

About Sue Urda and Kathy Fyler

 Sue and Kathy have been friends for 28 years and business partners since 1994. They have received many awards and accolades for their businesses over the years and continue to love the work they do and the people they do it with. As publishers, they are honored to help people share their stories, passions, and lessons.

Their pride and joy is Powerful You!, which they know is a gift from Spirit. They love traveling the country producing meetings and tour events to gather women for business, personal, and spiritual growth. Their greatest pleasure comes through connecting with the many inspiring and extraordinary women who are a part of their network.

The strength of their partnership lies in their deep respect, love, and understanding of one another as well as their complementary skills and knowledge. Kathy is a technology enthusiast and free-thinker. Sue is an author and speaker with a love of creative undertakings. Their honor for and admiration of each other are boundless.

Together their energies combine to feed the flames of countless women who are seeking truth, empowerment, joy, peace, and connection with themselves, their own spirits, and other women.

Connect with Sue and Kathy:
Powerful You! Inc.
239-280-0111
info@powerfulyou.com
PowerfulYou.com
PowerfulYouPublishing.com
SueUrda.com

Powerful You! Women's Network
Networking with a Heart

OUR MISSION is to empower women to discover their inner wisdom, follow their passion, and live rich, authentic lives.

Powerful You! Women's Network is founded upon the belief that women are powerful creators, passionate and compassionate leaders, and the heart and backbone of our world's businesses, homes, and communities.

Our Network welcomes all women from all walks of life. We recognize that diversity in our relationships creates opportunities.

Powerful You! creates and facilitates venues for women who desire to develop connections that will assist in growing their businesses. We aid in the creation of lasting personal relationships and provide insights and tools for women who seek balance, grace, and ease in all facets of life.

Powerful You! was founded in January 2005 to gather women for business, personal, and spiritual growth. Our monthly chapter meetings provide a space for collaborative and inspired networking and 'real' connections. We know that lasting relationships are built through open and meaningful conversation, so we've designed our meetings to include opportunities for discussions, masterminds, speakers, growth, and gratitude shares.

Follow us online:
Twitter: @powerfulyou
facebook.com/powerfulyou

Join or Start a Chapter for
Business, Personal & Spiritual Growth

powerfulyou.com

Are You Called to be an Author?

If you're like most people, you may find the prospect of writing a book daunting. Where to begin? How to proceed? No worries! We're here to help.

Whether you choose to write your own book, contribute to an anthology, or be part of our Wisdom & Insights book series using our QuickPublish Formula™, we'll be your guiding light, professional consultant, and enthusiastic supporter. If you can see yourself as an author partnering with a publishing company who has your best interest at heart and with the expertise to back it up, we're the publisher for you.

We provide personalized guidance through the writing and editing process. We offer complete publishing packages and our service is designed for a personal and optimal authoring experience.

We are committed to helping individuals express their voices and shine their lights into the world. Are you ready to start your journey as an author? Do it with Powerful You! Publishing.

Powerful You!
PUBLISHING
Sharing Wisdom ~ Shining Light

Powerful You! Publishing
239-280-0111
powerfulyoupublishing.com